Political History of Latin America

Political History OF Latin America

RONALD M. GLASSMAN

fW **Funk & Wagnalls**
New York

320.9
G

The author is grateful to The American Geographical
Society and The Rutgers University Press for
permission to reprint quotations appearing in
his text.

Printed in the United States of America

Acknowledgments

I should like to acknowledge the great debt that I owe to those who patiently worked with me over the years.

First of all, to Arthur J. Vidich, without whose inspiration this work never could have been conceived. His continuing dialogue with me and his patient rereading of the manuscript constantly reinfused vitality into my work, and his incredible ability to analyze coolly the unanalyzable continually opened up unknown dimensions which had to be explored. And to Ira Glasser, whose ongoing discussions, debate, support, and ability to pinpoint and circumscribe an idea filled me with an ever greater desire to penetrate to the heart of my subject matter, I owe an unpayable debt.

Then, too, I must thank Laurence and Caroline Raphael, who helped make the language, form, and ideas of this work more precise and readable.

Finally, let me make mention of the entire intellectual atmosphere of the New School for Social Research—a miracle of European (especially German) metaphysics and scholarship, existing as an exotic and magnificent island in the sea of American specialization. Special thanks should go to Carl Mayer, whose lectures and seminars make Max Weber's works dynamic and contemporary and alive. And also to Peter Berger, who opens up a whole intellectual world with his sociology of knowledge approach; and lastly to Aaron Gurwich, whose work epitomizes the philosophical foundations upon which the New School rests.

To ARTHUR J. VIDICH

Contents

Foreword

This work attempts to create a sociohistorical structure in which the apparent chaos of political events in Latin America may become meaningful.

Heavy reliance was placed upon the Weberian approach to social structure and social reality, including such concepts as classes as carriers of distinct social realities, the elective affinities of classes, class interactions, legitimacy systems, transitional legitimacy systems, and other Weberian constructions.

This kind of analysis has never been extended in depth to any of the underdeveloped countries, although some rudimentary attempts have been made in studying the Middle East and Africa (see Halpern and Apter). No attempt to apply this model to Latin America has been made at all.

It should also be mentioned that this work on Latin America is part of a larger work which attempts to extend the Weberian model of sociohistorical analysis beyond the origins of capitalism in Europe toward a more general model for the understanding of political institutions and institutional transitions generally. Much of this larger manuscript is complete, but it is as yet unpublished.

The model developed in this work begins with a structural-historical description of the emerging society in Spain during the "reconquest" epoch. A meticulous description of this epoch and the social structure emerging from it is given, for my first point is that the social structure developed in Spain during those "reconquest" years—with all its strengths and weaknesses, peculiarities and typicalities—was transferred whole to the new continent.

I continue with a careful description of the different courses which Spanish and Latin American history took as the two developed independently. The basic difference discussed is the consolidation of the kingship in Spain and the creation of a centralized, bureaucratized, legitimized state structure there, while the diffusion, disintegration, and breakdown of the bureaucratized, legitimized stable structure took place in Latin America.

A section then follows describing the process of conversion of the Latin American empire Indian, non-empire Indians, and Africans into the social structure which the Iberians had developed in their similar struggle against the Moslem empire. Great detail is included at this point. Key differences and similarities between the New World and the Old, the Moslem and Indian empires, and Spanish-Moslem, Spanish-Indian relationships, and their ramifications are pointed out.

A structural model of what I call the *semi-feudal* social structure of Latin America and "reconquest" Spain emerges as the dominant model of analysis. A description of the creation of semi-feudal private estates follows. The many ways through which estate-building occurred are taken up. A description of the semi-feudal estate-building class and its fusion with the ecclesiastical estate-building class is presented. The emergence of this semi-feudal "knightly" and priestly class as the dominant class in Latin American society is one of the basic structural elements of this work.

A constant comparison between this semi-feudal model and the true feudal model of Northern Europe appears. The ramifications of the differences between these two models is brought out.

The first basic difference between them was the failure of the semi-feudal system to create a system of order in the countryside. This left the countryside far more anarchic than the true feudal countryside had been and created a situation much like quasi-feudal warlord Asia after the collapse of the Asian empires. This semi-feudal social organization had, as permanent features of its partially anarchic structure, (a) permanent, professionalized bandits operating outside of the jurisdiction of the estates, (b) expanding, feuding private empire-estates not linked to each other in any kind of vassalage system at all. (Even in Spain there was some attempt at vassalage linking, though the bond was never reciprocal as in Northern Europe.)

The second basic difference between the "reconquest" Spaniards and Latin American social systems and that of Northern Europe was the divergence in the kinds of cities

which they created. The Spanish and Latin American
cities have within them elements of the capital-city model
of the Moslem empire where the cities were controlled by
the aristocratic and bureaucratic upper strata of the realm,
and elements of the city-state model of Italy where the
knightly aristocratic families competed for political power
in the open arena of the new politics of these independent
city-states. The cities of Northern Europe, on the other
hand, were bare market-cities run by an emerging independent set of commercial classes, unthreatened and even
protected by the knightly aristocrats of the countryside
who, for structural-historical reasons, found it more ad-
vantageous not to enter these cities (see Schumpeter and
Weber).

The Spanish and Latin American cities—like those of
Italy—became involved in a violent struggle for power
when the lords of the countryside entered them on a
permanent basis. What ensued was, at first, interclass
warfare, then intraclass clan and family feuding, and
finally, since the battles dragged on inconclusively, no
total legitimation systems emerged. Anarchy then ensued,
in which all the classes—lower and upper—became involved in the struggle for power, and in which naked force
and the purveyors of naked force—professionalized soldiers and thieves—became intimately involved. Another
result of these city struggles was the inhibition of the
commercial classes in Spain and Latin America, which
had begun to flower as lavishly as those of Northern
Europe.

The final description given is of the great divergence of Latin American history from that of Europe—and even from that of Spain. That is, the description of the linking of the Latin American semi-feudal estate class to the world raw-material market, and its subsequent accumulation of a large supply of capital.

The irony of the situation for the development of Latin America is profound, for the commercial classes dwindled as the semi-feudal classes obtained a permanent source of capital which sustained them and insured their power, while their European counterparts were being cut off from capital and their power usurped by the commercial classes.

Prologue

Latin America has remained an insoluble puzzle to most of its students. The political process in particular has confounded scholars for many generations. Yet, if Latin America is placed in its historical setting, its pieces melt into a totality, its structure emerges as a defined pattern, the puzzle becomes a picture, visible for all to see.

So let us begin with history, and let the structure emerge. But one must begin at the beginning, and the beginning is Spain. Spain, with its fusion of imperial-Moslem and feudal-Visigothic social structures. Spain, with its emergent bureaucratic kingship. Spain, with its splendorous cities and regional parliaments. Spain, with its Inquisition. Let us begin at the beginning.

The Divergence of Spanish History and Social Structure from That of Feudal Europe

PART I

The Divergence of Spanish
History and Social Structure
from That of Feudal Europe

1

THE SEMI-FEUDAL MILITARY ARISTOCRACY: THE INCOMPLETE VASSALAGE SYSTEM

Some Spanish scholars become very indignant and protest mightily against any comparison of the Spanish baronage with that of other European lands. Their Middle Age, they say, does not correspond to the medieval era in other lands of Europe; the term "feudalism" does not fit the Spanish social organization of that epoch. Spanish feudalism began amid the collapse of the Roman state, as it had elsewhere in Europe, and was preceded by the conquest of its indigenous inhabitants by the northern European tribes. Yet, where the crumbling of the Roman empire in Northern Europe led to Charlemagne's attempted reconstruction of that empire, in Spain this five-century process of movement from Holy Roman overlordship and relative anarchy to an indigenous, highly structured feudal system was cut short and interrupted by the Moslem conquest, which reimposed, instead, an urban-centered tribute state resembling the period of urban-centered imperial structures rather than a feudal structure.

The Moslem urban-centered empire lasted for over eight-hundred years! Here is the first great divergence of Spanish history from European history generally.

The Visigothic overlords retreated into the hills of northern Spain *before* the true feudal system of vassalage hierarchy had developed, and lost completely any sense of fief-manorial structuring of the countryside.

The Visigoths remained unconquered, although their lands had been taken by the Moslems, and formed leagues of knights—allied knights, never in any clear vassalage hierarchy—and, up until the reconquest began, elected kings in the ancient fashion in prefeudal European style from among the members of the council of allied knights.

Since it never developed the feudal fief-manorial structure the countryside remained in a semi-anarchic state, never completely controlled by the Moslems or the Visigoths. The Moslems demanded and got tribute from, improved and directed, agricultural areas, but never imposed tight control upon them. Land tenure and production were fluid, rather than rigid as under true feudalism.

Though the Moslems did enter the countryside and did engage in agricultural production on a large scale, yet, as in all urban-centered empires, the Moslems tended to concentrate their power and residencies in the cities, which they constructed with great rapidity. Each area had its capital city, each conqueror his personal palace-city.

Thus, where the rest of Europe (though Italy later diverges) was rapidly becoming *de-urbanized* and establishing an orderly *rural-subsistence* structure, Spain was becoming *highly urbanized, and its rural areas remained unstructured and politically anarchic.*

THE POCKET IN THE HILLS

The Moslems were stopped by the French at the Pyrenees, and therefore consolidated their empire to the south, but never were able to eliminate the large pocket of Visigothic knights and their entourages in the mountains.

These knights and their followers lived as pirates—raiding, and being raided by, the Moslems—*in contact with France, and through France, with European feudalism* and European ideas for three hundred years.

These ideas and institutions gleaned from France interpenetrated with the Moslem ideas and institutions to produce a social structure resembling the Moslem more decisively, but shrouded in the ideologies gained from France.

THE FORGING OF THE NEW "SPANISH" IDENTITY

But in the meantime, during these years in the hills, the grand dream, of course, was reconquest of the lost lands, power, and prestige. And in those years the doctrine which became *the* unifying doctrine of this ever more fantasied dream was Christianity—the unifying force of the Holy Roman Empire and the unifying force of true feudalism itself.

It should be kept in mind that the indigenous Iberians were still not intermingled with the Visigothic conquerors —there were no "Spaniards" yet.

The creation of the Spanish identity and ethnic unity took place during the three-hundred-year sojourn in the Pyrenees. The Visigoths and Iberians merged into one people, and Christianity became the unifying factor among the fractionated, only partially enfeudalized, populace outside of Moslem control. The Visigoths and the Iberians became one—the Christian-Spaniards—their opposition to the infidel Moslems welding their identities.

Thus, a *Spanish*, superregional, superlingual, Christian identity emerged during this period, and symbolized opposition to the Moslems.

"The reconquest took on the aura of a crusade during the ninth and tenth centuries,"[1] * and Christian symbolism—the symbols of the new fused Spanish identity—became the spirit that animated the newly created "Spanish" populace.

"In the ninth century, according to legend, word spread that a bright star had come to rest over St. James' lost tomb in northwest Galicia. . . ."[2] The reconquest had its unifying mythology. Having created a unified identity, it now needed a unified land area to house itself. A tribe had been created, tribal territory had to be regained.

* Superscript numerals refer to Notes (see pp. 289–293).

THE RECONQUEST OF IBERIA FROM THE MOSLEMS

Step by step, the kings conquered the land from the Moslems; they distributed immense domains, dignities, revenues, and subjects to their military leaders. To be sure, these donations and rewards gave rise to a powerful, a formidable aristocracy; but the origins of the feudal system are more complex than this, for in Spain "the wealth that was the reward for the warrior attached him to the Prince who was the author of these favors; but an obligation of this kind bound only the donatory. There was not that reciprocity of duties between vassal and suzerain that appears to have been a characteristic of French society in the middle ages."[3] Instead of being protected by a *reciprocal* contract, the vassal was covered only by the privileges (*fueros*) granted by the prince of the place where he lived.

Besides, in other countries, the feudal tie was both real and personal, whereas in Spain the relations of subject and sovereign, of vassal and suzerain, were above all *personal*, and therefore noncontractual, fluid, temporary, and shifting.

"The customs of neighboring France influenced Spanish society to borrow some features of no particular importance. The *titles* of duke and marquis were of foreign importation. But Spain never knew that maze of jurisdiction and fiefs, and that hierarchy which ascended from the humblest gentlemen, through a series of lords, vassals, and suzerains, to the king, the suzerain of suzerains."[4]

The military nobles "could renounce the obedience due a king without other ceremony than that of sending to him one of their men to announce the fact: 'Sir, in the name of such and such . . . I kiss your hand, and, henceforth, he is no longer your vassal.' "[5]

RAMIFICATIONS OF THE SEMI-FEUDAL SYSTEM

No fief-vassalage systems of permanent duration arose in Spain. Therefore, *a unified, orderly, stable military protective system in the countryside never emerged.*

Because of this, banditry existed in the Spanish countryside to a frightening degree, and travelers and—most importantly—*traders* in the land were inhibited from easy movement. Trade was thus somewhat inhibited and sectionalism, privatism, regionalism, and separatism fostered.

Things got to a point where each of the private knightly empires, including the cities and their incorporated surrounding areas, began acting as separate nations. They charged *tolls* for travelers who crossed their boundaries, detained travelers for search, and engaged in piracy. One can see that under such circumstances internal trade would necessarily be inhibited to some extent, and therefore that the growth of a merchant class would be slightly retarded.

It should be remembered that the Moslem epoch—a

period of many centuries—was a period of thriving trade in which a large city-dwelling merchant class had developed (of Moslem, Christian, and Jewish origins in about equal proportions). Therefore the period after the reconquest was a period in which a great amount of trade and a large merchant class were to be found. But from this period onward began a slow, but steady, decline of trade and the merchant class itself, beginning with the rural semi-feudal anarchy and ending with the Inquisition, which expelled the Jewish and Moslem merchants, and the discovery of the New World, which allowed for the bypassing of internal trade in Spain.

Another characteristic of this semi-feudal social structure that emerged in Spain was that pillage by the semi-feudal military nobility became common,* for the pattern of land expansion did not take on the feudal pattern of vassalage addition, but instead took on the pattern of extended conquest—which meant, not just the military defeat and subjugation of the weaker knight by the stronger knight, but direct occupation of the *land* of the weaker knight. The pattern resembled more the conquest of one empire by another than feudal vassalage accrual, since it included pillage, pirating, and general destruction of the possessions of the defeated knight. This was *not* the case under true feudalism. Since true feudalism was basically the protective system of a rural-subsistence society, and there really was nothing to take, whereas in

---

* As in the warlord system of the Orient during the seventeenth, eighteenth, and nineteenth centuries.

Spain there were the great treasures left by the Moslem civilization wherever a conquering knight turned.

Since there was no real military order, the cities did not grow in a milieu of military protection as they had elsewhere in Europe,[6] but instead had to form military leagues to protect themselves against the constant pillage of the anarchic semi-feudal "warlord" system.

Therefore, another characteristic of semi-feudalism was that the cities began to develop more in the Italian style as militarily *independent* cities allied one with another. At first these city military leagues were strictly *defensive* in nature and sought only to protect the cities from the excesses of the semi-feudal military nobility, and to protect and facilitate trade. But, the military leagues resulted in the cities seeking to extend their own territory as conquerors in competition with the semi-feudal military aristocracy.

The countryside became, then, a melee of competing groups all seeking the empireship of given territories, and all ruling these territories, not as interconnected fiefdoms, but as separate private empires.

2

THE NEW SOCIAL ORDER OF THE LATE RECONQUEST PERIOD: SLAVES, LORDS, AND WOULD-BE LORDS

LORDS, WOULD-BE LORDS, AND THE NEW "SPANISH" IDENTITY

Class origins had become slightly blurred in the battle against the Moslems, and heroes and clever manipulators of all classes could be knighted for brave actions in battle or other "useful" actions. Since this situation of reconquest and heroism lasted for centuries, the Spanish class structure developed certain peculiarities.

The possibility of (1) heroism in battle, (2) conquest of privately controlled lands, and (3) piratical and bandit acquisitions of wealth, produced a situation where every man could become ennobled, and where enormous numbers of men did receive honorific titles or the power that comes from territorial control.

Therefore, a new feeling began developing as part of the newly welded Christian-Spanish identity. That is, that each man had the *dignity of a knight*—that every

11

man was a nobleman. The spirit of the *hidalgo* (the knightly one) became part of the new Spanish identity being forged by the reconquest. Travelers from other lands noted that the poorest Spaniard acted with the gestures and thoughts of a member of the aristocracy, dignity being the key to their actions.

"The number of simple gentlemen was considerable. Certain provinces, such as Biscay, and certain towns, such as Simancas, made this claim *for all their sons*; a comfortable living and residence in a place *exempt from taxes* and enjoying liberal local "privilege" [*fueros*, or charter of privileges granted to a Spanish province by the ruling prince of the area] were sufficient grounds for assuming the title *hidalgo*.[1]

The struggle against the Moslems had developed in the people a "sense of dignity; the *habit of bearing arms*, and a distaste for manual pursuits."[2] This is the knightly elective affinity pattern. This knightly pattern with all of its details and ramifications became established in Spain as the personality pattern and social cynosure for everyone. (This pattern partially occurred in the Italian city-states, but not nearly so completely as in Spain.)

Another factor which militated toward the spread of the attitude of the *hidalgo* was the fact that "nobility could be transmitted from father to child. Bastardy was not regarded as a cause of shame."[3] This custom was derived from the Moslem urban-centered empire, and was typical of bureaucratized, concubine-slave, open mobility, urban-centered societies, as opposed to the closed-class, feudal-agrarian societies of the rest of Europe.

A simple acknowledgment sufficed to place the bastard on the same footing as the legitimate child.* In any case, being a "lord" carried with it not merely a set of personality characteristics, but also a positively privileged status involving economic, political, and social rights and exemptions.

"A mass of financial and personal privileges was attached to the quality of nobleman, be he the most significant or the poorest of simple gentlemen. *The first of these was exemption from all taxes, contributions, or imposts paid to the state or to the town.* In principle, he had preference over commoners in *the distribution of offices, of lay and ecclesiastical dignities.*"†

Thus it was that in the beginning the military nobility in Spain dominated lay and ecclesiastical offices in the emerging bureaucratic state structure. This was true later in all of Europe in its state-forming period, and held true in Latin America until the mid-twentieth century.

THE SLAVE-SERFS

The system of semi-feudal land relationships was far more severe than feudal relationships ever were, and can best be placed between true feudal *serfdom* and urban-centered imperial slavery.

"The lords domain was cultivated by serf-peasants

* This became the basis for the acceptance of the *mestizo* in Latin America.

† Modern-day Latin America and the relationship of the estate-holding class to the economic structure of the state may also be considered in this context.[4]

(*solariegos*) who made fixed payments. Their original condition must have been quite miserable. The original charter (*fuero viejo*) of Castile declared that "the lord can take the body of a *solariego* and all that he has in the world."[5] *This was slavery in all its rigor.*

The system of slave-serfdom persisted until the reign of Isabella (1474–1504), when, in her attempts to create a centralized state, she tried to destroy the divisive power of the semi-feudal, military nobility. She freed the serfs from bondage to the lords. The effect of this, however, was to create a vast dislocated class who gathered in the cities and expanded drastically the mob of dislocated persons who had already flocked there during the first years' disruptions in the battle against the Moslems.

These mobs of dislocated slave-serfs contributed to the hatred of the Jews and Moslems and eventually were drawn off into the New World, thus removing the potentially most revolutionary class from the cities.*

THE DISPOSSESSED WOULD-BE KNIGHTS

It was, however, impossible to reduce to slave-serfs "the valiant colonists who, following in the footsteps of the soldiers, pushed into the plains recently wrested from the Moors."[6] These men were allowed to leave the soil when their lot became too rigorous and look for a more humane master. The lord was not allowed to prevent their de-

* See the French city communes during the French Revolution 1750–1800; see also the English lower city classes during the English Revolution 1600–1700; see also the United States' Northern cities in the 1960s.

parture; he could only "distrain the chattels that they were carrying away."[7]

Thus there was produced a large number of men who left the land looking for a *world without labor*, and looking also for their *reward* for fighting the Moslems— title and wealth were their dream.

Droves of such discontented, dispossessed individuals fled the countryside and flooded the Spanish cities. These men played a crucial role in Spanish history as they did in the English and French Revolutions. They were later to (a) take part in feuds that rocked the class-torn, ethnic-torn Spanish cities after the reconquest, (b) fill the ranks of the new paid professional army of the centralizing state, (c) make up most of the mobs that hurled hatred, jealousy, death, and dislocation upon the Jews, and (d) make up the bulk of the adventurers and *conquistadores* who would spread the Spanish domain to the new continent.

THE NEW CLASS STRUCTURE

The Spanish class structure came to be made up of a dwindling slave-serf population, a declining knightly-military aristocracy, an emerging but weak class of city merchants, and a vast class of dislocated ex-serfs seeking aristocratic status and privileges. This latter class was, in essence, in search of title, land, and slave-serfs.

There were three roads open to the non-knightly dislocated ones in their quest to become part of the aristocracy:

(1) Heroism and loyalty in battle—first for five centuries against the Moslems, later against the American Indian empires. The reward for heroism was usually an honorific title, but—in Spain—often without land or serfs. In fact, there grew up great numbers of Spaniards claiming titles and the aristocratic deference patterns that went with them, but holding no lands or serfs in the countryside.

Men of this condition were quick to realize that the New World, with its open lands and Indian populations, might provide the lands and serfs which they felt were owed them.

In Spanish America the rewards for heroism in battle almost always consisted at least of a gift of land (*caballería* or *peonía**), if not always serfs to work such land. The word spread quickly to the landless dislocated ones.

(2) The process of private fief expansion was actively engaged in by the old lordly class and its new members in Spain. However, in Spain this process followed a pattern closer to private empire creation rather than feudal extension as in Northern Europe. Vast private domains were cut out of the blood of knightly struggles. Vassalage accrual was not the goal in Spain, as it was in Northern Europe; empire was the goal. Thus the semi-feudal rather than the true feudal system of land tenure became typical in Spain.

* The *peonía* consisted of enough land to support one family; the *caballería* was slightly larger.

This process was carried over into the New World by Old World knightly aristocrats and became the model for land acquisitions and tenure in Latin America. This model is unique, for it is neither feudal nor mercantile, but semi-feudal—that much more anarchic and fluid system that evolved in Spain during the reconquest period.

(3) Banditry and piratical practices in the countryside became common in war-torn reconquest Spain, and the new semi-feudal order encouraged rather than prevented such activities. This, too, was carried over to the new continent.

Thus, by the fifteenth century, the class structure had become fluid in Spain. The easy access to title and land led to a blurring of the boundaries of the old knightly aristocratic class. In fact, the title "rich man" began to replace the title "knight," and the upper class began to be made up of anyone who either controlled great landed wealth or great amounts of monetary wealth in the cities.

This amalgamated upper stratum of conquering knights and rich merchants came to be known as Grandees. But the social style of this upper stratum, instead of developing toward the merchant style and mercantile wealth which occurred in Western Europe later, developed toward a courtly style as in Italy, and for similar reasons.

The title "rich man" brings us to a discussion of Spain's city classes, their enormous increase in wealth and power, and their progression into the upper strata of Spanish society.

3

THE STRANGE TURN IN THE
HISTORY OF SPANISH CITIES

THE ORIGIN OF SPANISH CITIES AS MOSLEM
CAPITAL CITIES*

The Moslem empire was a typical urban-centered empire.
That is, the king of kings and his entourage of civic and
military followers were housed at a capital-city site from
which they ruled over and guided the affairs of the entire
empire.

The original capital of the Moslem empire was Damas-
cus. However, the king of kings—the newly created Mo-
hammedan Caliph—built a new capital at Baghdad. Baghdad was the original capital center for Spain, but local
control grew, and new capital cities were constructed in
Spain, the last great capital city of the Moslems being at
Granada.

The more fractionated the Moslem empire became in
Iberia, the more each little, separated territorial ruler built
his own capital, so that there were dozens of great capital
cities by the end of Moslem rule.

* The Visigoths had had some capital cities left over from Roman
times, but these fell into disrepair and were either rebuilt by the Moslems
or left to disintegrate.

18

With some exceptions, the cities were the most important centers of Spain, being the capitals of regions that comprised towns and villages subject to their jurisdiction. This pattern of cities as capitals for politically separated regions was also transferred to Spanish America and was a crucial factor in the emergence of the Spanish-American social structure and social style.

RAMIFICATIONS OF THE CAPITAL-CITY ORIGINS OF THE SPANISH CITIES AFTER THE RECONQUEST

Since they were originally *capital* cities, the Spanish cities, unlike the bare market cities of the north, housed great treasure and beauty. Luxurious living standards were carried over from the Moslem period. Great palaces and mosques were converted into luxury quarters for the rich town-dwellers after the Christian conquest.

In short, the most splendiferous, the most luxurious, the most desirous areas to exist in Spain, were the cities.

Therefore the Spanish conquering military empire-builders in the countryside cast jealous eyes at the treasures and way of life not yet in their grasp as they languished amid their less luxurious, less exciting rural empires. They desired nothing less than the full possibilities of living lives of luxury—as befitted conquerors—as displayed in the former Moslem capital cities. And hadn't the Moslem conquerors set the precedent for such a style of life?

And now, with the reconquest completed, there stood

these great cities beckoning to the new conquerors to live out the style of life of those who had formerly been their masters. Compare this situation to that of Northern Europe where the knights scorned the little frugal, dull, ugly, coarse, market-cities and preferred their far more luxurious castles in the countryside.*

But, the Spanish cities did not only have a Moslem empire capital-city heritage. . . .

THE SPANISH CITIES AS MARKET-CITIES

During the period of the reconquest—which lasted for almost five centuries—these formerly Moslem capital cities had become relatively *independent* of either Moslem or Christian control. Since they passed from the military control of the one to the other so many times over the hundreds of years of intermittent struggle, neither side came to control them. In order to preserve law and order, these cities were forced to develop control over their own affairs since the present conquering group might be ousted at any moment by members of the other side (or even by personal enemies of the conquerors on their own side).†

Since both the Moslem and Christian military nobles were dependent upon the trade, goods, production, and

---

* Until the 1750s when Vienna, Paris, London, St. Petersburg, and other cities became large capital centers of kingly, centralized states.

† Shown by the history of fratricidal disputes on both sides during the war years, as in the story of El Cid, for example.

monetary resources of the cities (such as artisan production of the implements of war, clothing, and money to pay their partially professional armies*), both encouraged and allowed the great independence and growth of these cities, just as in Northern Europe.

Thus the Spanish cities during the centuries of the reconquest had come to develop like, and more and more to resemble, in *political and social structure*, the independent market-trading cities of the north.

EARLY CITY ADMINISTRATION[1]

Government by Lot: Amateur Councilmen

As was typical of all newly separated incorporated cities, the first thing done was to cast lots for the distribution of the municipal offices among the different wards, an ancient electoral system,† wherein those chosen by lot served as volunteer governors and administrators for a short fixed term. The cities were divided into quarters (parishes)‡ that divided the municipal functions among themselves by lot.

These temporary amateur governors convened in a meeting called the council (not unlike a council of elders in a hunting or agricultural society, but without the clan base, and without permanent tenure).

---

* Discussed later.

† As in the Greek city-states in their earliest period; or also the North European market-cities in their earliest period.

‡ The parish, originally a religious unit, became a civic unit, as in English cities during their early period of development.

The sovereign rights of the newly chartered cities belonged to the town council.

Government by Election: Professional Politicians

The system of government by lot proved unwieldy and inefficient as soon as the cities grew larger in population and complexity, and, as was also historically typical, yielded to a structure wherein more permanent, more professionalized members of the towns held office for longer time periods. Government by lot, and amateurism, yielded to elected "representative" government by professional politicians.

THE COUNCIL OF REPRESENTATIVES TAKES ON A PATRICIAN CHARACTER[2]

The wealthy merchants had always had a voice beyond their numbers in the town councils of the European market-cities (and in the Greek city-states) due to their high status and great economic power. But when government by lot was replaced with government by elected politicians this influence became more direct and increased significantly. Elections were controlled through financing, gift-giving, economic blackmail, and other manipulations. Candidates for office were restricted by economic qualifications such as specific properties,* wealth, or landed property. The various districts, then,

* Ability to produce a horse, or arms, or wear certain clothing.

had their representation limited to those who qualified.

Once in office, politicians were financially inhibited from achieving their attempted goals, bribed into altering their position, and generally courted and controlled by the wealthy merchants outside of, as well as within, the town council.[3]

As the cities got larger, it also became necessary to appoint a vast coterie of men to bureaucratic posts which were too numerous to fill by election. Here, these bureaucrats (*procuradores*) "were not chosen by the people;"[4] they were named by the city council of elected representatives. But since the city council by this period "did not possess a democratic character"[5] due to the overweighted influence of the rich merchants, again we find that the bureaucrats were largely appointed at the discretion of the wealthier city-dwellers.

THE EMERGENCE OF THE THIRD ESTATE AND ITS REPRESENTATIVE COUNCILS AS THE POLITICAL ORGAN-OF-STATE: THE ORIGINS OF THE SPANISH PARLIAMENT

Castilian writers trace the origin of the "national" parliament (*Cortes generales*) of the Castilian monarchy to those councils of the Gothic empire, composed of prelates and lords, which gave their views on major religious and political questions.

This is typical for all Europe. The "national" councils were originally knightly and priestly councils made up of representatives of the knightly military orders and high prelates that convened in the presence of the king of the territory.[6]

As was typical for all Europe, "at first only the prelates and nobles were summoned, but in the middle of the twelfth century," in Spain, the secretary of the Castilians national parliament "(the *crónica general*) noted the presence beside them of the representatives of the cities (Cortes of Burgos, 1169)."[7]

"The representation of the clergy, regarded as the first of the estates,[8] had a completely *aristocratic character*. The abbots of the great monasteries, the bishops, and the archbishops held seats in the parliament by virtue of their titles.

"The nobility was represented by the . . . dukes, marquises and counts"[9]—the knightly military aristocrats.

In view of the fluid nature of the Spanish social structure during the years of the wars against the Moslems, it should not be surprising to note that "amongst the military aristocrats, also existed representatives bearing no knightly title, but only the designation 'rich man.' "[10] These were the *ricos hombres*, rich men, "who had no titles but possessed a regional jurisdiction,"[11] meaning landed estates and *paid* serf labor (tenant serfs).

"The deputies of the cities had seats beginning in the twelfth century; but the rights of the third estate in these great councils of the 'nation' were not clearly fixed until the beginning of the fourteenth century."[12]

"Originally, the number of deputies was unlimited."[13] All city-dwellers could carry their complaints to the parliament. However, since this procedure proved too cumbersome, "most of the cities entrusted management of their affairs in the parliament to their richer and more influential members."[14] Surprisingly, for those not familiar with the Spanish history of this period, "in what concerns *the development of municipal autonomy, Spain took the lead over other European lands.* The third estate wielded great influence there from an early date; the parliament (*cortes*) of Castile admitted the deputies of the towns to its midst a century before the communes were represented in the English parliament, and two centuries before Philip the Fair convolked the first French estates general."[15]

The form, structure, and style of the Spanish parliaments came to be dominated by the elective affinities of the third estate, as elsewhere in Europe, largely because financial matters came to dominate the affairs of the meetings, and the military and priestly aristocrats had neither the interest, the talent, nor the resources for such matters. Thus by the fifteenth century the parliament resembled more closely the town councils of the market-cities than the councils of knights and prelates of the feudal period.

The thirteenth and fourteenth centuries marked the most brilliant epoch in the history of the Spanish cities. However, unique events contributed to the ruin of the proud structure of municipal institutions.

What had developed was a network of trading cities

governing themselves independently through town councils dominated by rich merchants, and exerting a strong national influence through the national parliamentary councils. The cities also maintained their own militias.

This was a situation much like that in Northern Europe, but with one great exception.

4

THE GREAT DIVERGENCE OF THE HISTORY AND INFLUENCE OF THE SPANISH CITIES AND CITY CLASSES

The *physical structure* of the Spanish cities was the splendorous, luxurious shell of the Moslem capital cities, with their gardens and pools, gold and ivory, sculptures and mosaics, palaces and mosques.

Therefore, when the reconquest ended, instead of ignoring and exploiting the cities and snobbishly retreating to the private pleasures of the countryside as the North European military aristocrats had,* the Spanish semi-feudal nobility began, in great numbers, to take up residence in these formerly capital, now structurally market, cities.†

But residence in these cities by the great military grandees caused a major disruption of the pattern (which North European cities continued), for the independence

---

* Remember, too, that the Spanish and Italian countrysides are rocky and barren and not lush like that of North Europe.

† See Chapter 20 for the transference of this pattern to Latin America, and its reinforcement by the splendor of Mexico City and Cuzco as capital cities!

27

of those Spanish trading cities was immediately threatened. A new, powerful group had entered the walls of the
cities, and the tranquility of these market-cities—which
had maintained their complete independence and con-
ducted their own management of internal order through
the centuries of the reconquest—was to be rent asunder
by the ensuing events. The streets of the cities would soon
be stained by the blood of the competing camps, chaos
would replace order, and all of this—unlike Italy—would
eventuate in the subjugation of the previously proud cities
to the consolidating authority of the kingship.

RAMIFICATIONS OF THE MOVEMENT OF THE MILITARY NOBILITY TO THE CITIES: CLASS, FAMILY, AND FACTIONAL FEUDS

The rich merchants and merchant-gentry, who had purchased lands around the cities,* and to some degree, the
artisans, were the rulers of the cities. Their position was
thus threatened by the entrance of the knights into the
cities. They fought the military nobility in an effort to
maintain control over city affairs, and the military nobles,
of course, fought to wrest control from them.

"The *caballeros*,† after slowly moving in to the luxury
centers, formed an ambitious group which sought to win
full control for itself."[1] "In the fourteenth century this
class rivalry" between the knightly nobility and the

* This was a typical phenomenon in postfeudal England and Europe.
† Knights on horseback.

wealthy merchants "degenerated into brawls and riots at Cordoba, Segovia, and Sevilla,"[2] three of the most luxurious former capital cities (Cordoba being the original capital city of the early Moslem Spanish holdings.)

"The great lords . . . established themselves in the cities. There they waged armed struggle for power" (as in Italy); "they formed alliances"—parties, in the Italian sense; "attracted paid professional soldiers and criminals to their services, and transformed the streets into battlefields."[3]

The inhabitants of the cities were the victims of these struggles between hostile factions.* At Sevilla, a burned church, a devastated territory, a starving city, murders, testified to the cruelty and irreconcilable hatreds of the parties. "Unhappy Sevilla, bathed in the blood of thy children [residents] and *caballeros* [new resident knights]. . . ."[4]

"Galicia had been enslaved by lords who secularized the revenues of the church, terrorized the towns, and devastated the countryside. The villages (were forced to) pay tribute to these brigands of noble blood,† whereas the royal officials were never obeyed and had not managed to collect taxes since the reign of Juan II."[5]

Andalusia was a typical example of the kind of conflict that went on in the Spanish cities after the military nobility moved in.

---

* This also happened in contemporary Italian cities.

† The warlord situation in Asia after the collapse of the empires there was similar.

"Andalusia was a prey to two [cross-class] factions, one headed by the Duke of Medina Sidonia, the other by the Marquis of Cadiz. These powerful grandees . . . contended for power in armed struggle. Begun in 1471 in the streets of Sevilla . . . the struggle spread to other cities as well, for there were cross-city alliances" (or "parties," just as in Italy),[6] " . . . and attracted adventurers and thieves under its banners; it had fired passions, given license to every appetite, and provoked violent men to murder and assassination."[7]

5

TOTAL ANARCHY: SEMI-FEUDAL ANARCHY IN THE COUNTRYSIDE, CHAOS IN THE CITIES

A situation developed, then, where the cities degenerated into brawling chaotic enclaves in the midst of a countryside that was left without a system of order and protection.

"Murders, robberies, arson, injuries, riots, tumults, challenges, brawls, conspiracies"—such are the words that accumulate under the pen of the contemporary, Hernando del Pulgar.[1] "The countryside had become a desert," abandoned by the grandees and many of the peasants who now took up residence in the cities,* bandits terrorized the highways; a private person was in constant danger of his life."[2]

Thus, semi-feudal anarchy existed in the countryside, while Italian-style chaos and family feuding existed in the cities. Such was the state of affairs in Iberia before the kingly consolidation. And that consolidation itself was

---

* With the retreat of the Moslems, the disruption of irrigation techniques had made farming impracticable, and the peasants were forced to leave the land.

largely accepted by the contesting classes of the populace
because of its immediate and spectacular success in reducing and eliminating that anarchic situation. No such
kingly consolidation ever occurred in Latin America.

TOTAL ANARCHY AND A CHANCE FOR THE KINGSHIP

The city-dwellers did not fare well in their struggle against
the military nobility. They could not keep them from
usurping power in the town councils, nor could they
maintain even a semblance of internal order by yielding
concessions to them, for every concession to one knightly
noble led to jealousy and feuding by another, and every
concession to the knights in general led to counterplotting
by the displaced merchants and merchant-gentry.

Thus, the cities degenerated into chaotic, anarchic
bloodshed, and countless numbers of plotters and
counterplotters were murdered (to say nothing of inno-
cent bystanders). Professional criminals, murderers, and
thieves were encouraged rather than controlled, and grew
as a group in power and numbers.

Brigandage in the countryside also increased as the
military nobility left that countryside for the excitements
and political struggles in the cities. Therefore, trade—the
raison d'être of the cities according to the merchant and
artisan classes originally dwelling therein—was also
hampered and threatened with ruin.

The defensive military leagues which had protected the

cities from the excesses of the military conquerors all through the centuries of the reconquest now failed to produce the intended results. Something new was necessary if the cities were to survive as *market-cities* and if the trading classes, the merchants and artisans, were to survive at all.

There was only one force in the realm that the trading, city classes could turn to for protection against the domination and excesses of the semi-feudal military nobility, the kingship.

"The age of happy independence had passed; the towns must either obey the Grandees or submit to the King. The latter choice was certainly the wiser of the two."[3]

6

THE CONSOLIDATION OF THE KINGSHIP: THE END OF ANARCHY

"The crown derived most of its prestige from its own past."[1] Without going all the way back to the Visigothic monarchs who sought to revive in Spain the phantom of the Roman empire (but never got the chance as they did elsewhere in Europe), we may recall that after the defeat of the Guadelete (711) "the chiefs of the vanquished people had regarded the conduct of war against the Moslems as their first duty."[2] During these years of retreat, retrenchment, and rebirth, "the King was in all eyes the symbol"[3] of the budding national and religious aspirations of the newly forming Iberio-Visigothic national-"tribal" amalgam.

Yet the actual power of the kings was limited, for "under the Goths the monarchy was *elective*."[4] Ancient councils of "royal" clans elected the chief of the clan as council of clan heads; he was then designated king. This procedure continued for generations, "the bishops [of royal clan lineage] and the royal clan heads [knights], assembled in council, made and unmade Kings."[5] By degrees, "the choice was restricted to the members of a single family, but this rule was more than once set aside."[6]

34

When the battle of the Guadelete delivered Spain to the Arabs, the Christians who found refuge in the mountains of Asturias elected Pelayo, an alleged kinsman of Don Rodrigo, the last Visigothic king, as their ruler. For several centuries the nation being formed in the shelter of the mountains, and gradually advancing into the plains of old Castile, had the right to select its sovereigns.* These rulers were above all *military leaders* who could be deposed as punishment for incapacity or bad fortune.

It appears that beginning in the twelfth century the monarchy became hereditary. The Spanish kingship found itself, however, in a position of high prestige, but little power, as the reconquest period began.

THE KINGSHIP IN THE EARLY YEARS OF THE RECONQUEST

"Hardly had fear of the Moslems subsided when division broke out within the Christian camp."[7] The kings had leaned for support on the towns and nobility, but they had paid dearly for this aid.

A turbulent aristocracy claimed for itself all the royal prerogatives, including the rights of administering justice and making war. The military orders, which constituted the most energetic and warlike part of the nation, joined in the defense of their privileges at the expense of every other part, not excepting the king.

---

* In the way of the old military clans of North Europe and elsewhere. (Typical of this was the selection of King Saul, as reported in the Bible.)

"The towns, harassed by the lords, lacking adequate protection by the Crown, formed defensive brotherhoods that often were as much to be feared as the leagues of nobles."[8]

"Even the Priesthood made only too plain [their] determination to be exempt from the laws and the common burdens"[9] (such as taxation).

A number of kings tried to resist the towns and nobles in this period, and their fate shows clearly where the power resided.

"Alfonso the Sage [attempted to affirm] the divine right of kings. The lords . . . drove him from Castile and forced him to seek refuge among infidels."[10]

"Pedro III, who wanted to make foreign policy without consulting the cities and military nobles, was compelled by a union of burghers and nobles to . . . summon the parliament [estate council] every year, and extend the powers of the parliamentary courts of justice [*justicia*]."[11]

"The Condestable Alvaro de Luna who . . . raised all the great lords against himself . . . was defeated and paid with his head for his stern exercise of power."[12]

"On the plains of Ávila the lords proceeded solemnly to depose a scorned king and to proclaim as king his brother Don Alfonso."[13]

"In Castile, Pedro the Cruel or the Just . . . reigned terror and punishments on his Castilian nobles. The day came when he was abandoned by all and fell into the hands of his half-brother Enrique de Transtamara, who killed him with a dagger [1369]. . . . The reign of this dynasty, begun with a fratricide, was *the Golden Age of the Aristocracy.*"[14]

THE TYPICAL ESTATE-STATE[15] ALLIANCE BETWEEN THE KINGSHIP AND THE CITIES DEVELOPS

Then, as the infidels were dispossessed, the kings set about curbing the upstart nobles. *The chief weapons to this end were the strengthening of the cities, the enlarging of their middle-class population, and the creation of city militias.* The cities were granted new and more generous charters with extensive immunities and special privileges (constitutions, charters, *fueros*).

This zeal for the building of cities inspired "generous hospitality for Jews, Moslems, and foreigners"[16] as in Holland, Italy, Germany, and France during this analogous independent trading-city period. Toledo, for example, assigned separate districts to non-Spanish elements; within their sanctuaries, Jews were permitted to have their synagogues, Moslems their mosques. This happy tolerance prevailed, with fitful interruptions, until the fourteenth century.

Meanwhile, the powerful cities, with their "brotherhoods" for patriotic service (militias), and greatly expanding monetary wealth, buttressed the royal power against the quarrelsome nobles.

As everywhere else in Europe, the contest of power between the kings and the military nobility led to the inclusion of representatives of the town councils in the kingly decision-making process as part of its political structure (in payment for the fact that they had been supplying the kings with monetary and military support.) Such concessions became part of the inevitable debt which the kingship incurred by its heavy reliance upon the cities in their struggle against the military nobility. This political concession was universal throughout Europe.

Thus, during the years of the reconquest, the typical estate-state arrangements had been operating with the kingship weak, but attempting some sort of maintenance of itself through dependence on city money (in return for land and titles and political concessions to the city-dwellers).

THE EARLY DISRUPTION OF THE ESTATE-STATE SYSTEM IN SPAIN

(1) In Spain after the reconquest, however, the vassalage system was in total chaos, and individual conquerors ruled individual lands. The knightly orders were in such disorder that no representatives were chosen or sent with any consistency to the emerging national parliaments (national estate councils*). The knightly brotherhoods were ripped apart by the semi-feudal independent character of land tenure, and thus the role of the military

* All of the European parliaments grew up as estate councils in the estate-state postfeudal period.[17]

aristocracy—as a class—in the estate councils became at first diffuse, and finally ephemeral, thus weakening its position in the centralized state which was to emerge. (The members of the military class did not foresee this, because they were ruling with greater individual control in their own regional strongholds than any of their counterparts in Northern Europe ever did; moreover, they were, during the period of disorders in the latter part of the reconquest period,* in essence ruling the entire territory whenever they chose to exert themselves in a body.)

(2) Secondly, the movement of the military nobility into the cities greatly weakened the position of the cities, as we have seen, and created a situation of chaos and anarchy which gave the kingship a considerable advantage which it did not enjoy elsewhere, for *whereas in England and France the kings had to submit to the demands of the city classes* or risk total disaster (which was also true for Spain during most of the reconquest period), *after the reconquest, the cities had to submit to the king, or court disaster.* The kings of France and England were beholden to the towns, with little to offer in return but to (a) yield to political power demands, and (b) to dispense lands. However, in Spain the kingship had something else it could dispense in repayment of its debt to the city classes: *order* in place of anarchy. The kingship had *order* to offer for the cooperation of the city classes. For the alternative to the acceptance of kingly imposed order, for the city

---

* Thirteenth and fourteenth centuries.

classes, was not *revolution*—as it was in England and France and Holland—but ruin. The cities were not capable of controlling the excesses of the semi-feudal military nobility, who had literally invaded them,* and they were not able to establish internal order within their own walls. Already trade was dwindling, and the city-dwellers were being eliminated from control of their own town councils.

Thus, to avert total ruin, the Spanish city classes accepted subordination to the kingship in a desperate attempt to maintain at least some of their privileges within the solidifying kingly state structure through the national estate councils.† As we shall see, they did maintain their influence for two more centuries before the *Inquisition* and the *trade routes of the New World* eliminated their last bargaining positions.

Thus, the factionalism of the nobles and the eventual encroachments by the crown brought to an end what had been the brilliant career of Spain's urban centers. An omnipotent central government, such as that which later emerged in Spain, could not long put up with the prejudices, pretensions, and liberties of the towns. *Morever, "order and prosperity compensated for the loss of autonomy."*[18]

---

* This never happened in Northern Europe—though it would have had similar results since the northern cities were no match in military strength for the knighthood.

† Under similar circumstances in Cuba—anarchy, chaos, banditry (foreign and indigenous), and bloodshed—it might be considered that Havana's middle-class city-dwellers yielded to Castro for much the same reasons.

The Spanish cities then, with no other choice open, traded their autonomy and national political aspirations for the political and economic order imposed by the subjugating kingship. "As its only memorial of that glorious past in which the cities formed veritable small republics," and capital cities for the surrounding territory, "modern Spain preserves a very zealous and narrow local patriotism, a faded image of the ardent passions and generous enthusiasms of a vanished time."[19]

THE KINGSHIP SUBDUES THE TOWNS AND INCORPORATES THEM UNDER ITS SOVEREIGNTY

Royally appointed officials took over the towns and ended the feuds between the knights and the city patricians. The kings intervened in municipal elections at an early date. "Alfonso XI first employed this policy of encroachment. To restrain the town councils, whose independent spirit annoyed him, he introduced into many towns . . . royal agents who presided over the courts and administered justice."[20]

Alfonso XI hit on the idea of perpetual administrators (*regidores*). At Madrid, for example, he named in 1346, twelve *regidores* royal agents who should hold office at the King's pleasure. He did the same in many other cities. The Catholic sovereigns (Ferdinand and Isabella) pursued the same policy. "They generalized the institution of *corregidor*, suppressed elections wherever they could, and arrogated insofar as they could the appointment of municipal magistrates."[21]

THE INTERNAL POLICE FORCE ("NATIONAL BROTHERHOOD") UNDER KINGLY DIRECTION AND CONTROL TAKES SHAPE

The kingship promulgated (on April 27, 1476) a plan of political organization. Money was provided by the city classes, and a "well-armed force under good commanders"[22] was provided by the kingship. "The jurisdiction of this new police force (*Santa Hermandad*—Saintly Brotherhood—usually called the 'National Brotherhood') extended to all territory of the crown," and though the cities provided the money for this venture, they were penetrated by this national police force along with the countryside estates.

The military nobility "who were interested in maintaining the state of anarchy"[23] which they had used so well to their advantage were naturally "apprehensive and annoyed to see the cities place all their forces at the service of the crown."[24]

THE SUBJUGATION OF THE NOBILITY

Through the creation of the national police force, the cities were permanently penetrated by agents loyal to the king. But the autonomy of the cities was not fully destroyed, and after all, the cities still controlled the sources of monetary wealth, even though they were being forced to give up this wealth in taxes to the kingship in return for the needed political order which the kingship, with its centrally controlled police force, was providing.

Thus the power of the cities was temporarily limited, and the alliance between the kingship and the city classes was temporarily renewed (as in the earlier estate-state period.)

For now the kingship, in league with the city classes— in order to completely eradicate the anarchy and restore total order—turned on the semi-feudal military nobility, who, after all, had *created* the anarchy in the countryside as well as the cities.

"The great, the true, enemy of the crown was the independent and anarchical spirit of the nobility."[25] Its opposition had continued for several centuries. The nobles hatched league after league without even securing their own interests. Their agitation devastated Spain.

But the power of the military nobility was soon to be curbed in the manner typical to the European situation— that is, through their alliance with the (now desperate) cities, the kings would raise enough money to create a paid professional non-knightly army. And the historical situation of a prolonged war needing centrally controlled military direction for a lengthy sustained period of time— the siege of Granada, last stronghold of the Moslems in Iberia—would allow them to consolidate and institution- alize such a force* as the main military force of the land.†

---

* Similar forces arose during the Italian wars.

† The French and English kings used the Hundred Years' War as the pretext for maintaining a permanent professional army financed by city

THE CREATION OF THE PAID
PROFESSIONAL ARMY

The Usurpation of Military Power
from the Semi-Feudal Military Nobility

"The Spanish army underwent a complete transformation under Ferdinand and Isabella."[26] Between the beginning and the end of their reign, its *armaments, tactics,* and *mode of recruitment* were changed. "The war against Alfonso V of Portugal (1474–1476) was a struggle that recalls the melees of the middle ages; but at the death of the Catholic sovereigns Spain possessed a truly modern army, composed chiefly of infantry and relying not so much on individual bravery as on the solidity of its battalions, the agility of its movements, and the skill of its leaders."[27]

THE CREATION OF A CLASS OF
PROFESSIONAL SOLDIERS

Expeditions to foreign lands (Granada, Italy, eventually the Indies), and *long-term* military tenure did not suit the "drafted" serf-peasant militiamen of the typical knightly-peasant army. Thus compulsory service was instituted during several long and distant campaigns. But this com-

---

monetary wealth. The Northern European kings used the religious Thirty Years' War in a similar manner.

pulsory service was made viable by recruitment from a new class of men, not from among the stable peasantry and townsmen as was the typical feudal setup, but from among the hordes of displaced peasants who had gathered in and around the cities, where they formed a *lumpen* lower stratum which had not yet fitted into the newly emerging postfeudal social structure still amorphous at this period, and in Spain, highly anarchic and chaotic.*

THE "BRIGANDS"

The desire for booty and glory, the lure of adventure, supplied a mass of volunteers from the displaced classes†— especially those gathered around the large cities and port-cities. The sovereigns gladly recruited these men.

These first paid soldiers—as elsewhere‡—became "attached to their standards and *henceforth wanting no other homeland than the camp.*"²⁸ *Military service tended to become a trade;* the Spanish cities poured into Granada, Italy, and America their noblest and their vilest elements.§

* The postfeudal French and English prerevolutionary periods produced the same *lumpen*, dislocated class. The Spanish reconquest was an even greater creator of dislocated masses than anywhere else.

† Who were unnecessary economically, due to land shifts, new agrarian imports, and the sudden crowding of the towns and cities.

‡ The same trend occurred in Italy, England, France, Switzerland, Hesse, and Prussia in Germany.

§ Many of the brigands were former knights and lords; the subjugation of the nobility by the kingship led them to seek the life of brigands in an attempt to recapture their lost empires and authority, as in the movement of Ponce de León and other noble brigands to the New World.

THE NEED FOR ARTILLERY

The use of artillery in the seige of Granada was necessary—for its high walls were well fortified, and these new
devices were available already in Italy (where they were
developed by Da Vinci.)

The use of artillery required central direction, however,
with a bureaucracy to manage the host of secondary
artisans and laborers necessary to transport, manufacture,
get ready, and operate these new machines of war. Since
only the kingship had the budding apparatus and position
to direct such an operation, *and* since the feudal military
aristocrats knew nothing of how to operate or strategically
employ such new weaponry, the latter thus were auto-
matically excluded from the direction of the long siege of
Granada. In fact Isabella, functioning as the Spanish
kingship, imported Italian technicians and military ad-
visors, whom she gathered under her own control and paid
personally, thus usurping the control of military direction
at the siege by operating through these personally chosen
foreign agents with bought loyalty owed only to the
kingship.

Slowly but surely, the kingship was building a military
apparatus superior to that of the divided factional, feuding, only partially vassalized, knight-peasant armies, and
was bypassing them in its creation of this militarily superior professional army.

"Isabella summoned blacksmiths and engineers from

Italy, Flanders, and Germany, she imported considerable quantities of gunpowder from Sicily and Portugal; she assembled a powerful artillery."[29]

"The service of the artillery involved a multitude of secondary services. To make munitions and equipment for the artillery, there were employed many blacksmiths, carpenters, sawyers, woodcutters, smelters, masons, stone-cutters who looked for stone quarries, and other stone-cutters who worked the stone, and diggers, charcoal burners whose job it was to make charcoal for the forges, and *espareras* who made ropes and baskets. And over each group of workers was an overseer who urged on the workers and supplied them with the things they needed for their task. Moreover, a great many carts were needed, and for each hundred carts there was an overseer, and under him artisans to whom he gave the equipment needed to keep the carts in repair. There were other artisans to make the gunpowder, which was kept in pits dug out underground by three hundred men assigned to guard them day and night." Thus, "the war of Granada revealed the power of artillery; but it was the Italian war which put on record the value and future of the *infantry*."[30]

THE CREATION OF THE PROFESSIONAL, TRAINED INFANTRY

The End of Private Knight-Peasant Armies

"Gonzalo de Cordoba . . . re-organized the Spanish infantry; now it could match its strength with the Swiss." The latter, formed in a square and protected on all sides by masses of pikes, advanced on level ground with an irresistible impetus; "they presented a compact resistance front, *impenetrable to a cavalry charge, and swept before them the mass of foot soldiers.*"

Thanks to these reforms and still others not mentioned, the Spanish army was first in the world for a century and a half. Yet it must not be pictured as a school of virtue, austerity, or discipline. It was often the refuge of gross and violent men, avid for booty and carnage. They were trailed by a horde of prostitutes. The sack of towns, murder, and rape were among their most agreeable diversions. Mutinies were frequent; arrears in pay led to terrible upheavals that endangered the commander's life, and did not spare his honor.

As later on in Latin America, "*many nobles enrolled in the infantry!* Whereas French gentlemen disdained infantry service" since they were true feudal lords, "Castilian and Aragonese *hidalgos* gloried in fighting amid the foot soldiers"[31] since they were already dislocated from their class, their land, and their fortunes. The Spanish aristocracy was aware that here resided the true superiority of the Spanish army. Neither the English nor the French nobility saw this, but had to fight and lose to find out this truth.

The growth of the navy as a major instrument of war also altered feudal class categories, for although the navy eventually became highly stratified, originally, in England, France, and Spain, it was a defeudalizing, professionalized corps like the infantry.

7

THE INQUISITION

THE SUBJUGATION OF THE CLERGY

The entire unity and identity of the conquering nation had been formed under Christianity, thus the cross became the rallying point of the "Spaniards."

It was natural, then, for the clergy to be powerful in a land where a struggle of seven centuries against the Moslems had heated religious sentiment to an extraordinary degree.

The clergy was instrumental in the reconquest and, with this leverage and their largely aristocratic background, became a specially privileged group. "The law of the Siete Portidas had *exempted* the regular and secular clergy *from all taxes*. As a result, extensive domains escaped all obligations to the royal treasury; every new acquisition, every property secured by legacy or succession, increased the extent of the property under mortmain."[1] The clergy were also skillful in evading municipal taxes, to some of which even nobles were liable. This angered the third estate in the parliaments and the local city councils.

RAMIFICATIONS OF THE GREAT AND EASY WEALTH OF THE PRIESTLY CLASS

"The clergy were not content with the immense domains with which the piety of subjects and kings had endowed them. The tithe secured for the church a part of the product of those properties which it did not possess."[2] In the reign of Charles V the burdens of the tithe became so heavy and so frequent that the deputies of the towns raised their voices. . . . From all these sources the Spanish Church became extremely rich (drawing a revenue of 476,000 ducados annually).[3]

"The wealth of the clergy produced its natural results: ignorance and immorality."[4] "The privilege of clergy grouped about the clergy a half-lay, half-ecclesiastical following who led a licentious life in the shadow of the sanctuary and who covered the most profligate activities with the cloak of religion. These tonsured clerics, dedicated to God by their parents from tenderest infancy and entered by them in the minor orders, scandalized even the laity, and made money by exploiting the basest passions. The monks showed no greater capacity to resist temptation."

"The manners of the secular clergy were no better. *Castile was the only land where under the influence of the prevailing morality the bastard of an ecclesiastic had the right of inheritance from his father in case of death 'ab intestate'!* Concubinage was a normal, recognized, accepted state of affairs" (emphasis added).[5]

THE UPPER PRIESTHOOD AS PART OF THE KNIGHTLY NOBILITY

The high clergy gave an example of laxity. The prelates were generally men of high birth who retained the manners of the world, and who remained great lords in the bishop's palace. Alonso of Aragon, bastard of Ferdinand and Archbishop of Saragossa, was succeeded in office by his natural son. These sons and grandsons of kings sought an exalted social station in the church; they would have no nonsense about living like monks of humble life. They had worldly tastes and passions, and even fought in the battles between nobles and kings, now on one side, now on the other, as knights leading troops.

"The lives of these warrior-pontiffs were anything but edifying."*

THE REFORM AND ITS RAMIFICATIONS

"But whereas the other churches of Christendome slumbered in blissful peace and put up with their vices till the day Luther's thunder aroused them and forced them to reform on pain of destruction, Spain, which in the 15th century had its own heresy in the form of Judaism, was led sooner to undertake the work of reform."[6]

---

* As in the Richelieu era in France.[7]

Even as the pyres were being lighted for the Judaizers,* Isabella strove to keep her people faithful to Catholicism by restoring to the clergy the prestige of good examples and good actions. Jiménez (a converted Jew!) was made the organizer and administrator of the purging of the clergy.

"Jiménez . . . was declared enemy of indifference and laxity."[8] He began to visit the monasteries, to drive out unworthy brethren. The evil was so deeply embedded that four hundred monks passed over to Africa and became Moslems. Jiménez did not retreat.

The reform of the clergy was accomplished. And "the principle credit for it goes to Isabella, who brought to the choice of bishops and other high ecclesiastical dignitaries the most scrupulous care, the purest considerations . . ."[9] The prelates were chosen among persons preeminent for knowledge and piety; *the great ecclesiastical offices ceased to be a monopoly of the aristocracy* . . .

"The tendency was rather to select the bishops from the *lower nobility and the middle class* (*city burghers*), thus bringing the former into its allegiance against the upper grandees or Ricos Hombres, and the latter into monetary alliance for payoffs of clergy titles and offices."[10]

Thus the kingship purged the aristocracy and gained control over the clergy, who, henceforth, became their political henchmen and hatchetmen.

---

* Jews who converted under fear of repression.

The Purged Clergy as Tax Collecting Agents for the Kingship

Another source of revenue manifested itself to the kingship—the clergy had been expert at extracting its tithe from the population. The kingship would now be able to make use of this talent to fill its own coffers, since the clergy were now acting as agents of the kingly bureaucracy, loyal not to Rome or the church, but to the kingship alone.*

The newly created clergy displayed great zeal in serving the interests of the treasury. "The Spanish Parliament [*Cortes*] of 1512 complained energetically of the preachers of the Crusade who, in the towns force the people to take up the said Bull as penance†; and if anyone refuses, they drag him around in shackles to hear their preachments, and thus prevail on him at last by force and threats to take up the said Bull [pay the tax]." Thus were the priests used by the kingship to raise money and frighten the townspeople into submission to the authority of the kingship. "The abuses continued, and the indulgences were entered under the heading of regular revenues."

---

* Because of the reproduction of this system in Latin America and its continuance by the Spanish-Americans after independence, the later Latin American revolutionaries (as in Mexico) hated the priests.

† The papal decree allowing the kingship to tax the consciences of the people, by penance for wrong thoughts, was perpetuated by the kingship even after the holy war against the infidels had ended.

These taxes became so oppressive to the populace, to the city-dwellers and merchants in particular, that the kingship surely would have provoked a revolt similar to that of England's of the 1600s had not two factors emerged:

(1) The Inquisition, by turning against the Moslems and Jews,* allowed the cities to usurp the money and businesses of the Jews and Moslems who had flourished within their midst for centuries. This temporary increase in the personal fortunes of the city-dwellers forestalled their revolutionary tendencies by reimbursing them. One plunder, as it were, paid for another.

(2) The unmerciful slaughter of the Jews and Moslems by the kingship and its priestly agents frightened the city-dwellers so thoroughly that any thought of revolt was quickly hidden, lest the devil be discovered in that unpatriotic soul and his body burned alive—in full view, in the town square—as the other devil-filled heretics had been.

Thus the need for revolt was temporarily reduced with the redistribution of the "treasures" of the Jews and Moslems, and instead of revolution, there was reimbursement, containment through terror, and finally, complete domi-

* "The Inquisition, Part II, The Purging of the Moslems and the Jews" is omitted here, but appears as part of a manuscript on Spain and Europe generally, to be published in the future.

nation by the kingship. The dwindling of the city classes as crucial classes in the newly emerging state was almost completed; it would take only the growth of an independent source of monetary wealth for the kingship from the new continent to complete the eclipse of urban power.

RAMIFICATIONS OF THE INQUISITION

(1) Fear solidified the power of the kingship:

(a) The city-dwellers had been both appeased and decimated by the expulsion of the Jews and Moslems: the Spanish city classes were appeased, but at the same time, the city classes as a whole were cut in half by the expulsion of the Jewish and Moslem members.

(b) The military aristocracy and its segment of the priesthood had been purged and crushed.

(2) The wealth (although the immediate material wealth remained) and skills of the Jews and Moslems were lost to Spain, leaving a crisis in:

(a) artisanship (which necessitated the importation of Italian workers),

(b) agriculture (the Moslem agrarian technology was withdrawn, so that the lands were left unirrigated and improperly fertilized),

(c) trade and industry (with the ensuing demise of the silk industry and decline of internal trade).

THE FINAL CONSOLIDATION OF THE KINGSHIP

The kingly consolidation had begun during the reconquest period, as we described earlier, but this process did not culminate until centuries later, under Ferdinand and Isabella.

The consolidation had begun in typical fashion through alliance with the city classes and their monetary wealth. The Inquisition then provided a unique and powerful weapon, by which all dissident or potentially dissident elements remaining in opposition to the kingship were either purged or appeased (appeased through the redistribution of properties and wealth previously owned by those who had been purged).

The church was purged of dissident aristocratic elements, and forged into an arm of the kingly bureaucracy. The "loyal" churchmen acted out the king's commands and became an even more formidable weapon of control than the national police force in the final subordination of:

(1) the nobility, whose lands were confiscated and whose chief advocates were punished with death or banishment —as "heretics"—at the hands of the kingly dominated inquisitional tribunals,

(2) the cities, whose Jewish and Moslem merchants and artisans were murdered in public or banished; and whose

too independent officials were frightened into subordination by this show of Christian-clothed—and thus unassailable—kingly ferocity.

The kingship was able to achieve the subordination of the cities and the countryside because of the desperate need for order during the terrible disrupted period of internal anarchy following the nearly completed reconquest, and was able to cloak its repressions under the guise of religion because:

(1) Christianity equaled patriotism equaled unity in the fight against the infidel Moslems, and the inquisitional purges seemed patriotic and pious acts, rather than terroristic ones.

(2) The church had grown *venal* during the reconquest. Churchmen had taken land, women, tribute, and engaged in all kinds of blackmail (through the confessional) to attain materialistic goals. These blatant antispiritual actions had shocked and outraged the populace at large.

Thus the aristocratically based priestly class was discredited, and the purge of the church through the inquisitional courts made the kingship (Isabella) look saintly and reverent and pious.*

Isabella righted the wrongs of the church against the

* Under the Reformation in Northern Europe (especially England), the kingships attempted to subordinate the aristocratic clergy; France's failure to subordinate the clergy was a cause of its eventual political problems.

people. The fact that she was a woman helped, for a
virtuous woman was like the pure virgin, a mothering
figure to God and all men.*

Thus the purge of the church by the kingship was
hailed by all of the populace, and the kingship was careful
to reappoint only men totally faithful to its cause. (It
obtained this concession of reappointment through military and moral blackmail against the Pope (the "venal"
Cesare Borgia.)

Since the *virtue* of the inquisitional court could not be
contested and furthermore was graced with the charismatic purity of the righteous, dynamic woman-king, Isabella, most of the populace believed fervently that the
church had been purged of venality and that only the
saintly remained. Therefore the judgments of these courts
against the knightly nobles and town patricians were
generally accepted outside the circle of friends of the
accused. Furthermore, since in the cities the Jews and the
Moslems were the first to be purged, this pleased the
other city-dwellers and gave them enough immediate
profit—and scared them enough since the victims were
publicly burned—so that they generally yielded to all of
the demands of the kingship, and became thoroughly
subordinated to the kingship after this. The final blow to

---

* It is crucial that she—a woman, a Madonna—carved out these tasks,
for she looked doubly saintly—another Mary—a holy mother punishing
her wayward sons and re-creating the purity of the church. The Spanish
family structure and the mother-son relationship, especially, must also
be taken into account. Similar considerations apply to Eva Peron and
the Latin American family structure.

the cities did not occur, however, until the overseas trade was monopolized by the kingship and the cities were thus bypassed as necessary trading institutions. But the *precedent* for such kingly monopolization was set in this period, for had the kingship not totally consolidated its power, and totally subordinated the city classes during this period of the Inquisition, it could never have gained a monopolistic hold upon overseas trade, it could never have excluded the city classes from controlling such trade, and it could never have maintained its political domination over the emerging nation.

In England and Holland where the city-merchant classes monopolized trade through their privately controlled trading companies, they cut the kingship out of the great store of overseas riches which the Spanish kingship made its own. In England and Holland the monopoly was reversed, and it was the kingship which became a dependent, weakened, dwindling institution. On the contrary, in Spain, with the Inquisition and the internal anarchy allowing for a total and terrible consolidation of the kingship (and thus a complete, centrally directed, bureaucratic monopoly on all matters of state, including foreign trade), it was the city classes—merchants and artisans and their institutions and elective affinities (the parliament, the city councils, the law, money relationships, trade, religious currents, intellectual currents and forms)—that became weakened and watered down and eventually disappeared. In Spain these institutions and elective affinities disappeared more definitely than in

Germany, where at least the seeds of the new artisan religion (Lutheran Protestantism) remained, and where the gentry, though military in origin, still aped the forms of the merchant-gentry to a great degree. Certain intellectual styles and other elective affinities remained firmly rooted in Germany (although growing in a very different direction than elsewhere). In Spain, they bloomed in one great burst (in the golden age just after the reconquest), but were eventually almost completely uprooted until the industrial era, when their bud appeared once again—this time to be destroyed before it had barely flowered.

The power of the military nobility as a class had already been bypassed by Ferdinand's professional army, used in the forty-year siege of Granada, then the use of inquisitional pressure and action totally destroyed any vestige of their independence as high-status individuals and further subordinated them to the kingship, so that by the end of Ferdinand and Isabella's reign, the nobility had been successfully drawn off their lands, had taken up residence in the cities, and their land had been taken over as crown lands.

Thus, the consolidation of the kingship in Spain was total. *Nowhere else in Europe was the consolidation of the kingship so successful or so complete:* not in Germany, where the Junker military-gentry class remained powerful, nor in Eastern Europe and Austria, where the consolidation was loose, and always partially anarchic and locally controlled.

After the Inquisition, the Christian city patricians, the

rich merchants, and the artisans had even greater wealth at their disposal than before. Although they were frightened and politically terrorized (risking death at the inquisitional court), and blackmailed as well by the kingship (with offers of the redistributed Jewish and Moslem properties in return for political docility), they still were important to the kingship as a source of wealth, a factor which helped them *to retain some political power,* except that they were temporarily too frightened to use it.

The parliament continued to meet and supply revenues, with the great difference that now, after the reign of terror of the Inquisition and the purging of the key, potentially revolutionary leaders of the city classes opposed to the crown,* the parliament became a docile rubber-stamp for the demands of the kingship.†

Previously, the parliament had been a spirited body making political demands—and getting them answered—in return for the king's revenue demands. But now it was reduced to a frightened, impotent, fund-producer for the growing bureaucratic state, content to reap the economic rewards of the redistribution of wealth following the inquisitional expulsions, and too frightened by the inquisitional courts, the national police force controlled by the king, and the encroachments of the military nobility to seek political gain for a century.

---

* Many city leaders went to the torture chamber, or were burned as supporters of the "infidels," or for "anti-Christian behavior," meaning anti-kingly-state behavior, of course.

† More so in Castile than Aragon, as Ferdinand's Inquisition was never as successful as Isabella's.

Perhaps one hundred years later the parliament and its city and commerical classes could have once again reared themselves and become a political force in the land; in fact, no doubt they would have, but for another set of unique historical events:

(1) after the Inquisition, the kingship was able—since it had temporarily crushed all opposition—to create a vast, efficient, technically superior bureaucratic state structure to bypass and circumvent the city classes and their law-producing estate council.

(2) This *total consolidation and bureaucratic efficiency of the kingship allowed it to monopolize the trade from the New World and develop its own, independent monetary base. Without the political wedge of being supplier of money to the kingship, the city classes became completely powerless,* lost all ability for usurping power, and disappeared as an independent* political force completely.

(3) It should also be mentioned that the expulsion of the Jews and Moslems ruined the internal economy; agriculture, industry, and artisan production fell off drastically. But the temporary influx of colossal wealth from the new continent allowed the kingship to ignore this loss (and thus *further* ignore the commercial classes), and buy food and goods from other European nations.

---

* City-dwellers, and lawyers especially, continued to staff the bureaucratic state, but no longer acted as a class for themselves, and did not exert any political power in themselves.

Temporarily, then, Spain became rich with goods as imports, but finally, after a century and a half of this, all the wealth from the new continent ended up in the hands of the supplier countries from which Spain was buying its products, so that England, Holland, France, and Italy eventually gained the wealth of the new continent, and Spain found itself with a neglected, ruined internal economy, and a reduced, apathetic, unproductive commercial populace, dissipated and circumvented commercially, and disappearing altogether politically.

But now, before discussing the "Great Discovery" and its ramifications, let us examine the centralized, bureaucratic state structure which preceded it and controlled it to the last detail.

THE DECLINE AND DEMISE OF THE SPANISH ESTATES GENERAL (PARLIAMENT) (CORTES)

Before the creation of the national police force and the inquisitional court, "the Parliament dared to ask of the sovereigns," and of each of them, their "royal word and pledge" that they would not name any person to their lawmaking council or their law courts (*audiencia*), except in the case of a vacancy. In extremely strong terms they demanded the annulment of certain acts.

But once the royal power had been consolidated, "formulas of devotion and obedience replaced those haughty protests."[11]

"The political decay of these assemblies, so clear under

Charles V, was already visible in the time of Ferdinand and Isabella."

"The sovereigns, assuming the offensive in their turn, subordinated the Parliament to the *royal council of justice* which they had organized."[12]

This royal council of justice was the key council among the many other bureaucratic councils which the kingship was to organize. All of these kingly bureaucratic councils together eventually made up the offices of the emerging bureaucratic state, and became the state structure that replaced the state structure of the estate-state. Thus, the estate council of the city classes as organ-of-state was bypassed in Spain—as in Germany—and replaced with a highly centralized bureaucratic state structure dominated by the kingship. But here, in Spain, instead of relying on a military gentry (and later a technically trained intelligentsia arising from that knightly gentry), reliance was placed, first (before the Inquisition), upon Jewish lawyers, then, upon city-class priest-servants of the kingship (agents of the king during and after the Inquisition), and later, upon secular Christian-born city-class lawyers drawn off from entrance into the parliament and into the central bureaucratic court structure, usually from the middling echelon of city-class residents rather than from the upper, rich patrician city strata whose members continued to sit in the now impotent parliament and whose political power was thus bypassed by the use of lower city-class members. Both secular and priestly lawyer-bureaucrats would carry out this subversion of the parliament because it was their only chance for upward mobility, and also because of their jealousy of the patricians who never allowed them to be seated in the parliament.*

Thus the lawyers (secular and priestly) continued to be the agents of the state, but *law charisma*, that is, the creation of law in a legislative organ-of-state, ceased to have any significance in Spain, and eventually, the legists became merely technically trained, bureaucratic experts— as in Germany—and government by bureaucratic decree —with all its surrounding ellective affinities—efficiency, nepotism, bureaucratic corruption, and red tape—replaced government by law and by law-making debating councils with all of its elective affinities.

THE KINGLY BUREAUCRATIC COUNCILS AS THE ORGAN-OF-STATE

The royal bureaucratic councils and officialdom began as part of the estate-state. That is, the kingship was designated as the fourth estate and allowed a limited (though ever extending) boundary of jurisdiction. This area of political functioning required a staff of officials just as the third estate needed its representatives and legists, and the first and second estates needed their military and priestly hierarchies. Thus, in the estate-state compromise, the king was accorded a certain number of functionaries. These

---

* It was these same middle, city classes and their country cousins, the middle merchant-gentry in England who backed Cromwell's dictatorship and pulled off the coup against parliament in the second phase of the English revolution.

early functionaries were kept almost as kingly servants at the court, but as the kingship consolidated completely, these functionaries, councilors, and officials became the backbone of a semi-independent bureaucratic state extending their jurisdiction and authority deeper and deeper into every area of life.

On the whole, the history of bureaucratic expansion is typical in Spain, even though the structure of the bureaucratic councils included certain unique characteristics, such as the monopolistic "House of Trade," the "Council of the Inquisition," and the "Council of the National Police Force."

THE THREE MAJOR COUNCILS

"The Council of Justice was composed in its majority of men of middling condition who, owing everything to the crown, could not be other than its docile servants."[13]

This council slowly usurped the legal functions of the local city councils, national parliaments, and parliamentary law courts.

"The Council of State was presided over by the King in person."[14] Its jurisdiction included foreign affairs. *"The aristocratic element was more strongly represented in this body than elsewhere."*[15]

"The Council of Finance supervised the administration

---

* See as typical all over Europe—see the role of the aristocracy in the foreign service—foreign policy divisions of all the emerging states of Europe—see Europe even today—especially England and Germany—but all of Europe—see also Schumpeter's protecting strata theory.

of the public finances"[16]—and eventually became the instrument of kingly monetary autonomy when expanded to include *The Council of the Indies.*

BUREAUCRATIC COUNCILS UNIQUE TO SPAIN

The Council of State, The Council of Justice, and The Council of Finance evolved from pre-existing organizations, the ancient estate-state councils with their special representation. However, special circumstances during the consolidation period of the kingship led to the creation, under Ferdinand and Isabella, of four new councils: that of the Civic Guard, or internal police force;* that of the Inquisition; that of the military orders, which brought to heel, under officials directed by the king, all of the private armies in the outlying territories; and that of the Indies, which had a monopoly of all wealth, trade, and administration of the Indies, which provided the support and independence for the growing kingship, and which made the bureaucratic state fully *autonomous* in the realm.

Thus, the first three of these unique councils—the councils of police or Civic Guard, the Inquisition, and the professional army—were the instruments of the bureaucratic consolidation under the king, and of his accession to total authority in the realm, while the fourth was the

---

* Today, Franco's "Civic Guard," the arm of control over internal affairs of Spain, is essentially the same in structure and function as the police force (the *Hermandad*—national "Brotherhood") of Ferdinand and Isabella.

instrument by which the kingship maintained that total authority for three hundred years.

The old estate-state offices and titles were retained; the merchant and military aristocracy remained in these offices and maintained their status, but lost power.

"The new administrative system made the ancient offices useless"[17]—what was the chief justice compared with the president of the Council of Justice, who directed the court police with sovereign power and could, on his own initiative, without an order from the king, cause the arrest of the greatest of great lords? The chief justice could, if he liked, regard himself as a great officer of the crown—and did, and commanded high status for a century—but in reality he was "only a high palace dignitary."[18]

Little by little even the aristocratically controlled high military dignitaries, were "reduced to the role of decorative personages in the royal entourage."[19]

" 'All is changed,' says Salozar [a notable authority on the Isabella era in Spain], 'What was once an office is now a dignity.' "[20]

TYPICAL BUREAUCRATIC POLITICAL PRACTICES DEVELOP

Nepotism, Graft, Tenure, and Competition for Bureaucratic Offices and Promotions

When the bureaucratic structure became the dominant governmental structure of Spain, having replaced the

parliamentary structure, all of the characteristics associated with bureaucracy—the good and the bad—began to
appear.

Efficiency and control increased, the state became far
more powerful and orderly, uniformity of procedure and
intent blanketed the land.

But also, the parliamentary characteristics began to
disappear. Justice by law, debate of policy, and independent economic activity diminished greatly, while the
bureaucratic vices of nepotism, red tape, tenure, and graft
began to penetrate the body politic and alter the style of
life therein. The dominating classes of society had been
slowly altered; thus the styles of life carried by those
classes were passing, and the new style of life carried by
the new class was beginning to make itself felt.

Even during Isabella's reign, the vices of the bureaucratic system (as well as its virtues, I should add) began
to become quite evident.

Here are some of the problems of that structure:

"They received presents or permitted their children and
wives to receive them; their subordinates also accepted
gratuities for acts of oversight or favor. On top of presents
and money that royal officials received from persons under
their jurisdiction, they squeezed out of their position all
the financial advantage that it could yield. The issuance of
diplomas and letters and the performance of acts of every
kind were burdened with fees that formed part of the
emoluments. Thus they raised the cost of transacting
business as their greed dictated."[21]

In fact, the situation became so drastically corrupt in

the early part of Isabella's reign that she personally tried to create a system of countermeasures to protect the populace. Pressure was put on her through the still functioning Castilian national parliament to institute such reforms.

THE ATTEMPTED "OMBUDSMAN" SYSTEM OF FERDINAND AND ISABELLA (1480)

With this end in view, "the sovereigns decided at the Parliament of Toledo (1480) to send out *investigative commissioners or inspectors* charged with seeing that the royal agents performed their duties and that the royal ordinances were executed."[22]

The commissioners visited the provinces and towns almost every year; they heard complaints against the bureaucrats and verified accusations. The administration of the towns was the principle object of their inquiry because of the parliamentary protests of the high city classes (now chafing under the political jurisdictional whims of the centrally directed royal bureaucrats).

These commissioners were not themselves to act as judges, but to indicate to the high bureaucrats (*corregidores*) the suits they should initiate and the wrongs to be redressed. This was similar to the system of bureaucratic correction and protections in modern Sweden.* The institution of *perquisadores* (commissioners or investigators)

---

* Such systems of bureaucratic redress are to be found in many postfeudal European countries and in some of the Asian bureaucratic empires, such as China, where the village headmen acted as advocates to the local mandarin bureaucrat.

enabled the central government to "watch over its own
agents and hold them to their duties,"[23] while providing
a cooling-off structure built into the system as a safety
valve against revolt for the influential and noninfluential
who felt wronged by the royal bureaucrats.

After the reign of Ferdinand and Isabella, however, this
system of bureaucratic redress slowly fell into disuse, and
for those wronged by the all-powerful bureaucratic state,
the only redress became flight to the New World—an
avenue of political and social redress taken by scores of
influential and noninfluential Spaniards from that point
on in Spanish history.

But the tranquility, the order, and the relative efficiency
of the bureaucratic state outweighed its disadvantages
during its early period. Order was what Spain had needed
—even if it was the order of a domineering, often des-
potic, kingly bureaucratic state—for in Spain, the feuds
between the city-dwelling knights and the city merchants
and artisans had disrupted the ability of the parliamentary
estate council to keep order. Thus there had been no
choice but to turn to the emerging kingly bureaucratic
state.

England, France, Holland, and Germany were faced
with the same problem a century later. The problem,
though the solutions to this problem varied from country
to country, was similar, though the historical circumstances and internal class balances differed.

Thus on the eve of the discovery of the New World, we
discover in Spain a kingship more powerfully consolidated
and city classes more disorganized and subdued than

elsewhere in Europe because of unique internal circumstances in Spain: (a) the semi-feudal anarchy and its aftermath, (b) the national police force, and (c) the national unification through the Christian-Spanish identity and its aftermath, the Inquisition.

Into this context of weakened city classes and a powerful centralized kingship comes the great discovery. The ramifications of the discovery of the New World at this particular period in Spain's history were enormous, for the effect of the discovery, coming at this time, was to reinforce structural events which had already sent Spain on a unique historical course. Furthermore, the structural solidification in Spain meant that a unique historical process was to be passed on to a whole new segment of the world, the whole of Spanish America.

"In founding the Spanish colonies, the primary object was not to foment the nation's trade and industry *but to increase the revenue of the crown.*"[24] In pursuit of this aim, the government accorded the greatest importance to the accumulation of precious metals. Instead of seeking to promote the relations between the colonies and the mother country, the government at the outset planned to make all trade a state monopoly. The state reserved profitable operations for itself, abandoning to private enterprise only such activity as involved great risks. The customs officers visited and maintained a careful watch over every ship that entered port. All foreign traders were excluded. "Foreign merchants were strictly forbidden to trade with the Indies."[25]

"The House of Trade, established at Sevilla, the chief port to the Indies, was the mainspring of the colonial enterprise, the indispensable go-between between the Indies and Castile.* Everything went through this kingly bureaucratic central point; not a single item left for America without having been declared to the House; nothing came from the Indies without being deposited in the House."[26]

THE "GREAT DISCOVERY" AND ITS RAMIFICATIONS

The historical facts of the discovery of the new continent are well known. The ramifications of the discovery are what are crucial here.

(1) The kingship developed a monopoly on all wealth, thus gaining an *independent* source of wealth. Through this, the cities and their national parliament lost their political wedge—if the king was not beholden to them for monetary wealth, then he was not beholden to them for anything at all. Therefore they began to be called upon for help less and less frequently, until by the end of the reign of Charles V (fifteenth century) the parliament was a pleading, whimpering, disappearing institution of state.

Therefore, the estate-state forms with their elective

* The province of Castile controlled all trade with the Indies, although most of the colonists were from the seacoast area of Andalusia.

affinities and style of life dwindled and disappeared in Spain, and only the all-powerful kingship remained.

(2) All potentially rebellious opposition to the kingship, in terms of the remaining military nobles, displaced peasants, and city-dwellers (who had made up the riotous mobs of first the feuds and then the Inquisition), was drained off—off to the New World to seek better fortunes. The kingship was left completely unopposed, for the remaining wealthy city classes had already been cowed by the Inquisition.

(3) The effects of the "Great Discovery" on the Spanish economy were profound.

The internal economy of Spain had begun to develop under Moslem tutelage. Agriculture was greatly improved through irrigation and other advanced agricultural techniques. A silk industry had been begun. Jewish, Moslem, and Christian artisans were encouraged in the cities and flourished during that period.

However, with the expulsion of the Moslems and the years of intermittent warfare, the internal economy of Spain had begun to decline. The silk industry fell apart when the Moslems were expelled from Granada. Agriculture began to decline drastically with the Moslem withdrawal. Artisan production was cut to one-third its previous production with the expulsion of the Jews and Moslems from the Spanish cities. Already at the period of the siege of Granada, Italian artisans had to be imported for various tasks. And let us not forget that during the latter part of the reconquest period the anarchy of the semi-feudal military aristocracy, and their subsequent invasion and disruption of the cities, had already seriously reduced trade and the power of the trading classes. Although the centrally controlled national police force had restored order, internal and external trade in Spain never fully recovered. Tolls still blocked the roads, and tithes and taxes still squeezed the merchants' incentive.

The Inquisition was the final blow to Spain's internal economy in that it expelled at least one-third or more of the wealthy trading class, the Jewish and Moslem merchants* of the wealthier trading cities.

After the Inquisition, then, Ferdinand and Isabella inherited an internal economy in shambles. Naturally, they would have tried to rectify this problem—as all European kings did (for they needed money for foreign wars)—by once more encouraging the growth of trade and the trading classes. Thus the trading classes and their institutions and elective affinities might have grown once again despite the expulsion of the Jews and Moslems, for they had in England (1450–1650) *after* the expulsion of the Jews, *but*, and this brings us back to our point, the

---

* The Jews and Moslems had no ban on usury, therefore they were the most prolific and successful merchants in Catholic Spain. Since Spain had no new religion, usury as a merchant activity, though engaged in, never gained high status as it did in the north after the Protestant Reformation graced these activities. (Italy parallels Spain in this respect.)

discovery of the new continent brought with it an endless
and incredible supply of riches in the form of precious
metals and stones. Therefore, at precisely the point when
all other European kings fell back upon the merchant
classes in their need for monetary wealth for external and
internal expansion, the Spanish kingship got a miracle,
the delivery of unbelievably enormous and endless sources
of wealth, with no strings attached.

Therefore, the Spanish kings did not have to encourage
the development of the *internal* economy, for they had
been blessed with an *external* source of wealth. Not only
did they *not* have to develop and encourage internal
economic development, but they *preferred* not to develop
it (as all other European kings would have preferred not
to), for this unpredicted blessing of wealth from the
Indies meant that the only remaining class of potential
political foes to the kingship could be reduced and ig-
nored, rather than courted and compromised with.*

Thus the Spanish internal economy was allowed to
disintegrate, and the Spanish commercial classes slowly
and imperceptibly began to disappear as a force in the
realm.

At first, because of the disarray of the Spanish internal
economy, it was cheaper for the kingship to buy *all* goods
from the more efficient producers of other European
countries; so the kingship did so. But then, seeing the
political (as well as economic) advantages of such a policy

---

* Here again, Spanish historical and structural development turned in
a different direction from that of Europe.

(that is, the eradication of their last remaining indigenous political foe), the Spanish kingship increased this policy of bypassing Spanish industrial and agricultural producers and greatly increased its purchasing from abroad.

For their part, the city financial, commercial, and artisan classes made no protest against this policy because enormous quantities of luxury goods at very cheap prices began to flood Spain as the kingship's policy of exchanging precious metals for foreign-made goods increased. Therefore they began to live a life of easy luxury without increasing their work efforts!

Thus the Spanish commercial and artisan classes drifted into the easy life of the golden century following the "Great Discovery." By the time they realized that their power base had been bypassed and their political power potential totally destroyed, it was too late. The kingship—independent and invincible—was supreme in the land, and the city commercial classes and their once vital institutions were merely voiceless ghosts haunting the carcasses of the once great cities.

8

THE TRANSFER OF THE RECONQUEST BATTLE TO THE NEW CONTINENT

Granada fell in 1492, but the battle did not end, for in the next fifty years the new Spanish professional army was transferred to a new front. The Moslem empire had finally fallen, the American Indian empires awaited their turn.

The discovery of the new continent did not cause a radical departure in Spanish policy; it merely allowed for the continuation of the same policies and techniques employed for centuries against the urban-centered infidel Moslems to be extended to the urban-centered infidel pagans!

The Spanish military nobility and professionalizing army, having fought the Moslems for hundreds of years, perfected their military technique to the utmost. By the time of the siege of Granada—the last stronghold of Moslem power in Iberia—the Spanish army had become fully professionalized and one of the most militarily advanced in the world. Again, the siege of Granada ended in 1492.

The Spanish professional army knew exactly how to

fight the American Indian empires since they had an organization similar to that of the Moslem empire. And of course, the Indian empires were much less well equipped in a technological and military sense. The Indian empires, it should be remembered, unlike the Moslem empire, possessed no horses, no swords, no armor, no catapults, no guns, no real fortresses. They fought on foot, exposed, with nothing but slings and arrows, whereas the newly developed Spanish professional army had fought against a superior foe for nearly a hundred years.

Also, just as they did against the Moslems, the Spaniards were able to set up alliances with disaffected Indian groups which had formerly been integrated into the tribute structure of the great Indian empires. They were also able to buy off regional leaders, just as they had in Moslem regions peripheral to the capital centers.*

Thus, the situation, even in its military beginnings, resembled the reconquest period greatly, and as such, can be seen as an extension, rather than a new direction for Spanish history. The ease with which the Spaniards conquered the vast new continent, and their efficient integration of this continent, with a minimum of colonization,† can be understood in these terms.

So, with little awe—for they had lived in the awe-filled shadow of the Moslem empire for hundreds of years—the

---

* See the *Saga of El Cid* for historical details on this in Spain. Cortez and other chroniclers are also sources on these actions in Latin America.

† The English never integrated North America so soon or so fully, even with a large colonization.

Spaniards relived a new "reconquest," with less men against a less militarily formidable foe, by holding the advantage of the elements of surprise and by default of the Indians' magical world view when confronted with events outside of its scope of reality.

THE REVIVAL OF THE SOCIAL AND REALITY STRUCTURE OF RECONQUEST SPAIN ON THE NEW CONTINENT

The kingship had subdued the forces of semi-feudalism in Spain, and created order where there had been chaos and anarchy. But the Spanish kingship was a long way off from the new continent, and the order which it had created in Spain began to disintegrate across the seas. The tides separated the Spaniards in the New World from an orderly, systematic, centralized state structure once more, and the sands of time eroded what little which had been preserved.

The years of consolidation and order in the kingly bureaucratic state were wiped out on the new continent; the years of the freewheeling, wide-open wealth and status-building off the reconquest period had returned.

In Spanish America, as in reconquest Spain, the possibility of (1) heroism in battle, (2) conquest of Indian controlled lands and treasures (Moslem land and treasure in Spain), and (3) piratical and bandit acquisition of wealth reproduced a situation in which every man could become ennobled, and where enormous numbers of men did receive titles or the power that comes from territorial control. The spirit of the *hidalgo,* and would-be *hidalgo,* re-emerged from the corpses of the Indian aristocracy, as it had once emerged from those of the Moslems. Land, slaves, and titles were available once again. The New World had opened the door to the Old. The past, stereotyped and idealized by those of the present, was to live on, in an exaggerated form, in the future.

The entire semi-feudal structure, with its (1) anarchy in the countryside, (2) urban-centered style-of-life, (3) regionalism and private empires, (4) spirit of heroic ennoblement, and (5) priestly involvement in worldly affairs—in short, the entire social structure of the reconquest period in Spain—was extended to Spanish America.

It is as if the reconquest was re-created in the New World, as if Spanish history were rolled back two hundred years, and allowed to flourish again in a new, more primeval setting.

And so they came from Spain, the dislocated ones who had crowded into the cities, the lords who had lost their lands, the priests who had lost their independence. And they gathered on the new continent, not to establish a new social order, but to re-create the one they had just lost.

The semi-feudal social order with its values of land and title and the knightly style of life which the Spanish kingship was slowly destroying, this is what the emigrants desired, this is what the emigrants created. Knightly conquerors, not merchant-settlers, landed on the shores of the new continent, and they set about with amazing rapidity and efficiency in their task of re-creating their familiar reconquest social order in the lands they came to claim.

The acquisition of knightly manors stocked with obedient serfs was every man's goal, to become lord of the fief was every man's desire. The knightly style of life had emerged triumphant in Spain—even though the knights had not—and "everyman an *hidalgo*" had been the cry that emerged from the conquest of the Moslems. That cry had been muffled in Spain by the spreading cloak of the Spanish centralized, bureaucratized kingly state, but now it echoed once again throughout the hills and plains of the New World.

"Every man a knight," this became the passion of the conquerors, it had been their passion as they conquered the Moors, but it had been frustrated. Quelled, but never extinguished, it had festered in the hearts of those denied its access. Now, the cry burst forth again, more powerfully because of its earlier frustration, more desperate because of its probable lack of success, more successful because of its knowledge of the past—more successful because of its distance from the crown.

Thus did the conquerors from Iberia attempt to establish a social structure derived from thirteenth- and fourteenth-century Spain, and thus did they succeed. For the forces of the vanguard of sixteenth- and seventeenth-century social structure innovating Spanish and European life at the time were too far away, too concerned with themselves, and the dynamics of the indigenous Indian empire social structure (so similar in structure and historical direction to that which was desired by the conquerors, and to that which they had conquered in Moslem Spain) had already laid the groundwork for such a system.

9

INTRODUCTION TO THE ORIGINS AND FORMS OF LATIN AMERICAN SOCIAL STRUCTURE

LAND DISTRIBUTION AND OCCUPATION IN RECONQUEST SPAIN AND LATIN AMERICA

In reconquest Spain, when lands and people were recaptured from the Moslems, they were given out as rewards to military, political, and economic leaders. Concessions were also given to foot soldiers and cavalrymen in the form of smaller plots of land to which no serfs were attached.

Over the centuries, an orderly system of land distribution and control had been developed by the Spaniards, so that by the time of the Spanish conquest of the new continent, they were the most experienced empire-builders of their day and had already worked out a relatively smooth system for the occupation, utilization, and incorporation of conquered territories and peoples.*

The *semi-feudal estate system with regional capital*

---

* Though this system—as we had seen in Spain—had glaring faults in it once the conquest was concluded, yet, as a system for initial incorporation and organization of conquered lands and people it was highly efficient.

83

cities was the system of land tenure evolved by the Spaniards. It resulted from a peculiar fusion of Moslem imperial, urban-centered ideologies and social structures with elements of the French feudal system. This fused system of urban-centered empire relationships and feudal relationships—which I call semi-feudalism—was transferred to the new continent. The details *in toto* of this accomplishment are the subject matter of the immediately following sections of this study.

Though urban centers were actually occupied first wherever they existed (in the form of capital cities of the Indian empires), and though cities were often built before semi-feudal estates were created or occupied, still it is useful to begin our discussion with the creation of these semi-feudal estates, for it was the creation and ownership of estates that formed the major thrust of early Spanish colonization. The conquerors' interest in the cities occurred only after the estates had been permanently created and the indigenous population pacified and utilized as a permanent class of negatively privileged serfs on these estates.*

An Overview of the Spanish System of Land Distribution and Occupation[1]

As in Spain, "Once the loose gold and other concentrated forms of wealth had been divided up between the conquerers and the king, the main method left to the king

* A sequence of events, again, similar to that which occurred in Spain.

for paying his "debts," on the one hand, and for consolidating his newly won domain, on the other hand, was *grants of land*. In New Spain, such grants were made on a lavish scale in several forms—all of which tended to reestablish the nascent institution of private landed estates.*[2]

The first and most important form of land distribution was a form which consisted not only of land, but also of serf-subjects who went with the land. This was called the *encomienda* (literally, the entrusted lands, "God given in trust of so and so"). "The *encomienda*, as developed in the West Indies and Mexico, consisted of an allotment of a certain number of villages and carried with it the right to collect tribute and to exact personal services (labor in the fields and household, etc.) from the Indians living in the district thus allotted. In return, the individual receiving the trusteed lands was strictly enjoined by law to protect the persons and property of his 'subjects',"[3] a typically feudal arrangement.

The system of trusteed serfs and private estates was a direct replication of the characteristic features developed in the semi-feudal organization of the large estates worked by serfs in Castile, "it fitted like hand to glove in the situation which the conquerers found already existing in the land of the Empire Indians."[4] As we shall see, it did not fit where empires were absent, such as in the lowlands and in the islands. In these latter areas it had to be

---

* Which had so recently been broken in Spain.

created through the importation of Africans from budding urban-centered kingly areas.

Where Indian empires existed, "in many cases, the Spaniards . . . simply took the place of the defeated (and all too often dead) Indian chieftain (or clan head or military aristocrat) and continued to collect the tribute and services which before the conquest had gone to the Indian emperor."[5]

"The individual allotments made to the *encomenderos* were often of very considerable size, embracing many villages, with populations totaling hundreds and even thousands of souls. . . . All the Spaniards could be lords or *caballeros*. Concessions and grants could be generously made on the new continent, for every man there was, in a sense, a *principality*.[6] Given the Spanish *hidalgo* ethic* and the just previous history of the destruction of knightly estates in Spain, it is not surprising to find that the Spaniards' craving for the knightly estate should transfer this zeal to the ready-made situation on the new continent. Nor is it surprising, therefore, to learn that "before the close of the first half-century of occupation a large part of the inhabited region . . . was held in *encomienda* serf-stocked, private landlordly controlled estates. . . ."[7]

But, "the *encomienda* was not the only form of land grant or the only way in which the seeds of private estate ownership were planted. The rank and file of the conquering armies (and later, anyone in royal favor) received outright grants of land, but without serfs."

* See my section on the Spanish character and the ethic of "every man an *hidalgo*."

"These grants (called royal favors), originally designed to reward the less important of those who took part in the conquest, and later, serving as bait for attracting colonists to New Spain,[8] were of two types: *peonías* and *caballerías*" (corresponding to the army ranks of foot soldiers and mounted cavalrymen).

"The standard size for a *peonía* was approximately one hundred acres, made up of various classes of land estimated as *necessary for the support of a single family*. A *caballería* was five times the area of a *peonía* and probably varied in individual cases from 500–1000 acres, depending upon the quality of the land involved . . ."[9]

The *peonía* and *caballería* are less important as land-institutions in themselves than as bases, as it were, for the accumulation and integration of more land and of tenant serfs and of the further creation of private landed serf-holding estates. For, "these grants were . . . in many cases a nucleus about which the recipients accumulated additional holdings either by appropriating adjoining Indian lands, by political marriage, by purchase, or by other means, fair or foul."[10]

Thus the crucial fact about these smaller land grants is that *they never became the basis for the creation of a small holding class of market-oriented, free farmers as was the case in North America. Instead, following the traditions of reconquest Spain, they became the base for a subsidiary class of aristocratically oriented estate-builders, who were anticipatorially socialized into the semi-feudal estate-lord model, and actively supported and emulated that class and its goals.*

All of the land grants in the Spanish controlled territories, then, tended to develop in the same direction, toward semi-feudal, serf-holding, landlord controlled estates. It is to the details of this semi-feudal estate formation that we now turn.

LAND RELATIONSHIPS IN SPAIN AND IN LATIN AMERICA

During the centuries of the reconquest of the Spanish lands from the Moslem empire, the Spaniards developed an indigenous system of land distributions and incorporation.

Through this system, grants of land and inhabited villages were entrusted to those who gained either military or political favor with the kingship, or to those who could control such lands as they had acquired through military force, even in the face of kingly opposition.

Under the influence of French feudal institutions, the form of these land grants and tenure came to approximate the French true-feudal model, so that fief and manorial relationships were copied and developed in the aftermath of the reconquest.

Large grants of land went to the knights of the realm (later to professional generals in the last stages of the reconquest),* to heroes, to high and influential priests, to monastic orders, to court politicians, and bureaucrats in high favor, to merchants who had helped finance the years of war, and to others.

* See Ferdinand's professional army of 1490, Ch. 6, p. 44.

Those receiving the land grants began by emulating the French-derived true-feudal model, but very quickly departed from certain features of that model:

(1) True vassalage links were never really forged in Spain, so that the manorial-subsistence military units had less the character of feudal fiefs than that of private empires, like those later to appear as warlord enclaves in Asia. Lacking the vassalage fief obligations, the manorial relationships took on a much more directly *personal,* rather than legal and traditional, character.

(2) As a result of this, the quality of the relationship between lord and serf also differed from that of the true feudal model in that the relationship—more personal, and less clearly delineated and restrained by any long developed, legal-traditional rules of interpersonal class relations —took on the character of a master-slave relationship rather than that of lord and serf.*

(3) Even this more personal, less structured relationship (in terms of the lord's obligations to other lords, and the lord's obligations and limitations in behavior in relations to the serfs) did not last, as the lords were drawn irresistibly to the pleasure domes of the still standing Moslem imperial cities, and *left* their private manorial estates for the luxury and excitement of these cities.

These luxury-seeking absentee lords left overseers and administrators on their estates as had the lords of the

_____
* Partly derived from Moslem institutions.

ancient Roman empire, who had likewise left their slave plantations to seek the pleasures of the great capital cities. These overseers ruled the estates as slavemasters had ruled the mines and estates of ancient empires (including, of course, the Moslem empire), thus reinforcing the slave-like quality of the serfdom.

The ramifications of this absentee landlord system of semi-feudalism were profound, in that (a) the absence of the lords from their private estates created anarchy in the countryside for it de-reified* the slave-serf populations from the lordly authority structure producing large-scale banditry, unrest, and dislocations from the manor, and (b) the slavelike, poorly defined relationship between overseer and serf created great wellsprings of hostility and rebellion in the enserfed populations.

This entire social structure with all of its ramifications was re-created on the new continent; and it is to the task of showing this—in all its complications and permutations—that we turn now.

However, it must be pointed out (though it will be spelled out carefully later) that certain significant differences occurred in the subsequent histories of the Spanish semi-feudal, city-centered social structure to distinguish it from the Latin American semi-feudal city-centered one:

(1) In Spain the emerging centralization of the king-ship—a phenomenon occurring throughout postfeudal

---

* The serfs no longer recognized the authority of the lords as legitimate.

Europe—restored order in the countryside by reincorporating the private knightly estates into a central bureaucratic structure from which they had been separated for centuries, and brought both the knightly and the priestly lords to heel under its authority.

(2) The presence of large numbers of Jews and Moslems in the midst of the new nation allowed for the hostilities of the downtrodden slave-serf populations and the dislocated city mobs to be turned toward the rich "ethnics" rather than toward the overseers, lords, priests, or kings. Through the kingly institution of the Inquisition, the public burning, flogging, expropriations, and dislocations of the Jews and Moslems served as an avenue for the displacement of the hostilities that might normally have caused revolution, rebellion, disobedience, or criminality within the body politic of the newly emergent Spanish kingly state.

(3) The Inquisition also accomplished a purging of the wealthier, more irreligious priests and the confiscation of their vast landed estates. The subsequent redistribution of these estates also accomplished a reduction in hostilities amongst the dislocated population, since much of this land went to non-knightly, peasant foot soldiers who had been dissatisfied to return to serfdom—and who often received honorific titles with the land.

(4) Most important of all, for those who received no recompense from either Inquisitional or bureaucratic

gratis, there was one more avenue open for mobility and escape from the negatively privileged status of slave-serfdom—that of emigration to the new continent and there, a chance to gain the rewards of status, land, and adventure that were closed off in the newly created Spanish state. Hundreds of thousands of dislocated, discontented serfs and lords and priests fled to the new continent, there to gain and re-create that which they had, or wished they had had, in Iberia.

In Latin America, as we shall see, though the Spanish semi-feudal, city-centered, reconquest social structure was re-created, (a) no kingship existed to centralize, bureaucratize, and reincorporate the private, personal empire-estates, (b) no alien population lived within its midst onto whom slave-serf hostility could be displaced,* (c) inquisitional confiscation did not lead to the redistribution of land to the lower classes at all (although it did to the commercial landless Spanish class, as discussed later), and (d) most importantly, no avenue of mobility, escape, and adventure existed to draw off the dislocated or the dissident populations.†

But let us first look to the re-creation of the Spanish semi-feudal city-centered reconquest social structure on

---

* Though the isolated village Indians were scapegoated wherever they could be, yet they remained outside of the social structure and negatively privileged, whereas the Moslems and Jews were at the center of the social structure and their positively privileged status made them easier targets for hostility.

† Puerto Rico and Mexico in the twentieth century are exceptions, with their emigrations to the United States.

the new continent, and develop its similarities with that superimposed upon the urban-centered Moslem empire by the feudally influenced Spaniards, before we examine further the differences and problems inherent in the emergent Latin American social structure.

 PART **II**

The Origins and Form of the
Latin American Social Structure

PART II

The Origins and Form of the
Latin American Social Structure

10

THE SYSTEM OF ENTRUSTED LANDS AND PEOPLES: PRIVATE OVERLORDSHIP AND SLAVE-SERFS

After the occupation of Spanish America, "the system of entrusted lands was introduced."[1] *The system was not new*, as stated previously, having been employed earlier in the reconquest of Southern Spain from the Moslems.

As first established in the Western Hemisphere, "the system of *encomiendas* or *repartimientos** consisted in the distribution of the Indians among the conquerors. To each colonist was assigned a certain chieftain† with his followers, and these were obligated to till lands, work mines, or carry burdens for the *encomendero*"[2] (the one entrusted with the lands and the people).

* Isabella didn't want slavery, just serfdom, therefore she changed the name but not the form of the land and people "gifts." *Repartimiento* signified a gift of slaves with no land-rights (usually for mining purposes). *Encomienda* signified a gift of land-stable serfs, an idea less repugnant to Isabella's Catholic sensibilities. She thus enjoined all gifts of lands and people, whether given as people alone for slavery purposes, as in the West Indies, or given with land. It was in this sense that she changed the name and not the conditions of the grants. Mine slavery was simply not specifically labeled as such, and only the term *encomienda* survived, though the practice of *repartimiento* slave-grants continued during the early colonization period.

† Exact description of chieftainship follows; see Ch. 12.

To the kings of Spain the system offered an effective means for subjugating the native inhabitants. It had effectively brought the conquered lands and people under Spanish authority, had given the invaders possession of the soil, and had provided them with labor whereby *they could live without performing manual work, which the Castilians regarded as distasteful* and which the climate of the tropics and the extreme highlands made almost impossible for them.*

"An *encomienda,* as the term was generally employed in the colonization of Latin America, was, then, a *grant of Indians together with the land they inhabited,* given by the King or in his name, as reward for services rendered in the conquest of the continent."[3] It was based on the theory that the conquered peoples of America were under an obligation to pay tribute to the king of Spain. This theory derived from the Moslem system of overlordship under which the Spaniards lived for approximately eight centuries.

This tribute the king farmed out to his soldiers as a recompense for the part they played in the conquest and to enable them to live off the land they were conquering (as they had in reconquest Spain).

However, one immediate difference occurred in the tribute system of the New World as compared to the Old,

---

* See Ch. 2 on the anti-manual-work, "every man a *hidalgo*" ethic of reconquest Spain. Note also that all the European knightly class disdained manual work, although the climate *was* conducive to it. See Argentina where the climate *was* conducive.

for *"since the Indians could not pay in coin,* the Spaniards were authorized to collect this contribution to the crown *in services* . . . consisting in military duty (in the extending conquests of other Empires and tribes southward and westward), in the mines, in the fields, in the houses of the newcomers."[4] Not that this sort of direct enslavement did not occur widely in reconquest Spain, for it did, but there is a difference of degree here. In reconquest Spain large numbers of Moslem military nobles, merchants, merchant-gentry, and even artisans and tenanted farmers had the wherewithal to pay tribute in coin and were allowed to do so, in view of their often superior prestige and technological skill as compared to the Spaniards'. In the New World the Indians of all classes had neither the prestige, the skills and, most importantly, the money* to acquire the freedom from manual services that was otherwise demanded of them. Thus a system of almost total slavery emerged on the new continent as the Spanish social structure was superimposed upon the newly conquered lands and peoples.

Efforts were made by the Spanish kingship (especially by Isabella, who was sympathetic to the plight of the

---

* Only the few emperors and highest princes had the wealth, but they were systematically murdered or imprisoned by the Spaniards as they were the only figures and symbols around which revolt could be fostered. The great Moslem emperors conveniently withdrew to North Africa so that the Spaniards never had to confront such a situation. Given the prestige of the Moslems as a higher civilization this never could have occurred anyhow, but the Indian emperors were considered pagans and were not accorded prestige.

newly conquered peoples, and the reformed churchmen, especially the Jesuit order), "to hold the *encomiendas* to their original character of a mere right to extract services in lieu of tribute."[5] But the authority was far away; supervision was in the hands of officials who, having ambitions and opportunities of their own, in terms of gain from the system emerging in the New World, were generally in sympathy with the colonists. Thus enforcement of such benevolent legislation proved impossible.

As *actually practiced in the New World,* "encomienda *came to be a form of slave-serfdom, mild or severe according to the character of the recipient* and the degree of faithfulness with which the royal decrees were carried out in a particular locality."[6] This is as it had been, at least to some degree, in reconquest Spain and should be distinguished from the "pure" serfdom of true feudalism on the Northern European manors.

CHILE: A TYPICAL EXAMPLE OF "ENCOMIENDA" LAND OCCUPATION

An example which illustrates how quickly and efficiently the Spaniards carried out their colonization policy is offered by the case of the colonization of Chile.

There, "on January 12, 1544, only three years after Santiago* had been established Valdivia† began the dis-

* Capital cities were built first, and served as a base from which *encomiendas* were doled out; but as mentioned earlier, these cities did not gain significance until after the estates were firmly established and

tribution of *encomiendas* just as soon, in fact, as his little band of Spaniards had been able to bring the region into subjection. Near Santiago, the only district as yet fully under the control of the Spaniards, sixty *encomiendas* were bestowed upon as many *conquistadores*, the other soldiers being assured that further grants would be made as the conquest progressed southward."[7]

"Before the death of Valdivia (1553), most of the Indians in central Chile, and in the northern valley oases of Capiapó, Huáscar, and Coquimbo as well as many groups in the southern forests about Concepción, Valdivia, Imperial Osormo, and Villarrica* had been distributed among the conquerors. A sufficient number of *encomiendas* was distributed (particularly from Concepción to Santiago and in the transverse valleys of the north) to establish the system as the basis of conquest and settlement in Chile."† [8]

SIZE AND STRUCTURE OF THE "ENTRUSTED" ESTATES AND THEIR SERF ENTOURAGE

The number of Indians comprising an *encomienda* varied widely. "Valdivia, for example, is said to have reserved for

---

the conquered populations reduced to serfdom. At this early point they were merely bases for royal Spanish political and military authority and ports of call for royal monopoly exports.

† Conqueror of Chile.

* Outpost settlements, military and religious.

† Some special conditions in Chilean estate-building will be discussed in Chapter 15.

himself some 1,500 natives at the time of the first distribution, and to have presented 500 to Inez Suárez and 400
to Jeronimo de Alderete, his lieutenant." Other *encomiendas* were much smaller, averaging perhaps some 50–
100 Indians. "In more populous areas, the number of
Indians included in an *encomienda* was usually far
greater. Valdivia, at a later stage of the conquest, took
some 40,000* for himself."[9]

In Mexico and other empire areas, "the individual
allotments were often on a princely scale. Cortes himself
was rewarded with a vast concession which included 22
towns (each with its surrounding lands), representing a
population of 23,000. The royal decree granting these
estates specified that Cortes should have the lands and
subjects, the woods and the pastures, all waters, both
running and standing, *and complete civil and criminal
jurisdiction—all the rights, in short, which belonged to
the crown itself in the aforesaid land.*"†[10]

Another example of the extensive grants made to Spaniards was the entire district of Tula, in the present state of
Hidalgo in Mexico. This district with its eight pueblos
and nearly 300 Indian families was held by the Duke of
Atrisco, one of the many Spanish noblemen fleeing the
kingship and its Inquisition who was able to re-establish
his lost Old World empire in the new continent.[11]

* He later lost these in an Indian counterattack.

† Thus a private semi-feudal estate was created. It should be noted that
the estate lords retained civic, military, judicial, and even religious
control over their serfs. In some places this lasted until the early
twentieth century.

SLAVE-SERF AND OVERLORD
The Forced Labor of the Newly Formed Estates

As the *encomiendas* became more firmly established, and as the Spanish conquerors secured a greater and greater hold on the land itself on which Indian labor could be employed, the system provided a means whereby newcomers might live with ease and comfort. "All the necessary manual labor was performed by the Indians."[12] The colonists loudly proclaimed that they could not possibly occupy the land and maintain themselves there except by means of forced labor. "The *encomienda* system thus provided the labor supply considered essential to the establishing of every Spanish colony."* [13]

The Duties of the Slave-Serf

The first use made of the *encomienda* Indians in the early years was for slave labor in the mines, and for soldiers, often shanghaied, who were used to carry out the extended conquests to the south. But, before many years had elapsed, especially after independence severed Spain from her lifelines to the mining monopoly, "the services rendered in the mines and the military service, which was no longer necessary after the pacification and incorpora-

---

* This same system existed in the Philippine Islands before the United States takeover.

tion of the indigenous peoples, had become of less and less importance than that in the fields."[14]

"In the agricultural tasks and in the care or flocks and herds the working conditions were much less oppressive than they had been in the mines,"[15] for this type of labor was familiar to most of the natives.* In addition, the relationship of lord ·to serf on rural estates was usually more benevolent than that between the miner and his overseer (capitán).[16] In fact, in contrast to the period of full slavery of the earliest years of the conquest, which had been necessitated by the dependence upon mining and also engendered by the normal excesses of newly conquering soldiers, there developed *a truly serf-lord set of relationships approaching that of manorial Europe,* but still retaining some of the overtones of the slave period. There emerged, in short, a set of relationships mirroring those of the semi-feudal estates of reconquest Spain.

A detailed list of the requirements made upon the Indians of a Peruvian estate has been preserved and shows the use made of the Indian service. This list specifies that "the Indians of a certain *encomienda* should provide 75 *pesos* worth of gold each year [as tribute], that they should make and deliver to their master a fixed amount of native cloth [as subsistence artisanry], that they should plant each year ten or twelve measures of maize and seven or eight of wheat, from which 400 measures of maize and 300 of wheat must be retained for the Estate Lord [as

* Though this was not true for the hunting peoples, as will be shown in Chapter 11.

subsistence lord-serf agriculture], while the Indians were entitled to any surplus produced and were obliged to make good any shortage."*

The *encomendero* himself was to "attend the threshing with oxen or horses on the threshing floor on his own account, but could call upon the Indians to help with his work."[17]

Furthermore, "the Indians were to supply each month forty fowl (half of them hens) for the house of the estate lord; forty arcobas of fish every year delivered to the lord's house; 30 eggs were to be brought to the master each Friday and each 'fish day' during the Lenten season, 4 pounds of fresh fish on each of these days; 250 lbs. of salt, 12 sacks of charcoal; lastly for the personal service of the estate lord there must be maintained a force of 12 Indians, serving in relays to tend to the cattle."[18] While the details of the services demanded varied with the needs of the Spaniards in the different regions, this listing may be taken as typical of the requirements in most of the Spanish colonies.

* Similar relationships existed in the economies of Rome, Greece, Persia, *et al.*

11

COMPATIBILITY OF THE SEMI-FEUDAL SOCIAL STRUCTURE WITH THE PRE-SPANISH INDIAN URBAN-CENTERED EMPIRES

When the *encomienda* system was inaugurated among the hunting peoples of the islands and tropical coastlands, it did not work, for the Indians either refused to work or, enslaved and driven, died working.

However, when the system was applied to the inland urban-centered Indian empire and agricultural peoples, for whom it had been unintentionally designed since it was derived from the conquest of just such a structure, it had admirable success and achieved the expected structural, social, economic, and political results.

Both structurally and ideologically,* the system was alien to, and impossible to establish upon, a base of hunting peoples. Only where a compatible structure, ideology, and, in short, total reality existed, could the Spanish system be created.†

---

* Not that these things are separable—see Weber, Mannheim, and Marx.

† This is one of the keys to the understanding of the transference and evolution of political institutions, wherever they interpenetrate through-

Thus, when the semi-feudal lord-serf system of estate-holding was introduced in the West Indies, it met with

out the world. A more complete statement of this principle—and this is an old principle—will be formulated later on in this author's projected work, "The Evolution of Political Institutions." It will be explicated with the details of these political transferences and attempted transferences, and through the actual evolution of the political institutions in all the areas of the world, with special reference to the underdeveloped countries.

This problem is especially applicable to the liberal dream of the recreation of British and American parliamentary institutions in the underdeveloped countries, and may be the key to the understanding of the evolution of political institutions in the underdeveloped world today. For, as we shall see, where the Spaniards attempted to set up their semi-feudal system upon peoples without a compatible reality and social structure, such as on the islands and in the tropical lowlands among hunting peoples, they failed utterly in this attempt.

Other examples of the failure to transfer political institutions on non-compatible bases, which will be discussed in this and the total work, are:

(1) Simón Bolívar's disillusionment at the failure to transfer the United States-French-British parliamentary state structure to Latin America.

(2) Sun Yat-sen's bewilderment at the failure to transfer United States institutions to China and his subsequent movement toward U.S.S.R. Leninist institutions.

(3) The former colonial powers' disappointment in Africa when parliamentary institutions collapsed after their military and political withdrawal.

(4) The United States' disappointment in Cuba with the electoral system after the Spanish-American War.

(5) The United States' failure in Southeast Asia, South Vietnam, and South Korea to establish actual (rather than merely visible) United States political institutions even while her military and political presence was still maintained.

(6) Eastern Europe and Germany before World War II also failed in their attempts to establish Western European political institutions.

(7) The cases of India, Israel, Uruguay, Chile, and Ecuador need special illustration as possible exceptions to the rule of compatibility in political transference. These do not present a real threat to the compatibility principle, as will be shown in Chapter 20.

little success; in fact, "when first introduced in the West
Indies, among hunting and early agricultural peoples, the
repartimiento or *encomienda* system had practically depopulated the Islands within a few decades."* But in the
conquest of the Mexican and other urban-centered empires, the Spaniards had at once been led past the coastal
lands and had established themselves upon the temperate
uplands. Here they found late agricultural and urban-
centered empire peoples, "who for centuries had occupied
and tilled the fertile *balsones* and valleys of the plateau
and prized the soil as their chief possession." Furthermore
the Spaniards found in the Indian empires† a *system of
tribute already established,* by which the emperor and his
associated military nobles had drawn revenue from conquered districts. "The existing system was well suited to
the needs of the Spaniards, and replacing the . . . military nobles in political control, 'they collected the tribute
formerly paid to the . . . emperor.' "1‡

---

* This caused the importation of African urban-centered peoples in the
lowlands and to the islands, discussed in Chapter 15.

† Aztec, especially.

‡ This was typical wherever a conquering people took over the
administration of another empire. The Turks did this with the Arabic
empire, the Mongols with the Chinese, the Arabs with the East Indians,
the Romans with all those that they conquered, the Greeks with the
Persians, the Spaniards with the Moslems, and then, with the American
Indians.

THE FAILURE OF THE "ENCOMIENDA" SYSTEM IN THE LOWLANDS AMONG THE HUNTING PEOPLES; SUCCESS IN THE HIGHLANDS AMONG THE EMPIRE INDIANS

In one important respect the plan adopted in the highlands differed from that previously employed in the West Indies. In the earlier case "the unit of allotments in the *encomiendas* and *repartimientos* had been the individual chief and his followers* having been assigned to each Spaniard."[2]

Because these hunting and early agricultural peoples had no real *permanent settlements* (the way the Moslems or empire Indians did), they had to be alloted by clan or band with a chieftain or headman or clan elder as head. This was a far more disruptive process than had occurred in Spain, since these peoples were then uprooted from their typical routine.

By being uprooted from their daily routine, which had consisted almost entirely of food production, the subject peoples failed to produce their own minimal subsistence because the Spaniards diverted them from this pursuit into forced labor in areas nonproductive of food.

Having no surpluses of food, nor any surplus of *people* available for outside, nonsubsistence tasks, as empire peoples did, they began to fail to reproduce themselves,

* Headman of the band, or head of the council of clan elders (*cacique*).

for to do so they would have had to spend their full time at subsisting.

These peoples, especially the Carib Indians on the islands, and also along the tropical coastline, actually died out, at least as pure biological and cultural units. They survived only insofar as they intermarried and became integrated into the new semi-feudal lowland plantation structure that was later to emerge.

However, in the case of the empire and agricultural Indians, though many of them were diverted into mines, house slavery, and soldiering (and these *never returned* to their clan villages), there were surpluses of people since the villages were still intact. Enough men stayed behind to continue to produce at least a subsistence level of food, and they continued, thus, to reproduce themselves.

As a matter of fact, *the administrators of the Indian empires had always drawn soldiers and miners and slaves from the villages.* And their population, given its techno-logical level, could bear this drain, for the density of population was higher in the late agricultural, early urban-centered periods in comparison to the sparse population of the hunting people.*

Life, then, was not as greatly altered for these empire peoples as it had been for the less technologically ad-vanced peoples of the lowlands. The empire Indians maintained themselves and survived, and the Spaniards were able to superimpose a stable social structure upon

---

* A contrast in population density in the fifteenth century also existed between the United States plains and the Mexican highlands.

this compatible structure already existing in the highland areas.

The key difference between lowland and highland Indians, was that *"among the sedentary Indians the unit of place was able to be substituted for that of kinship"** [3] and used exactly as it had been used in reconquest Spain. "Allotments were made, not by headmen (*caciques*), but by villages," because there were permanent villages.[4] "Each rewarded Spaniard received a village or a group of villages as his *encomienda*."[5] This produced a much more permanent and less disruptive kind of takeover.†

Within a brief period after the conquest, the *encomienda* system, *"became a system of land tenure. . . . The colonists soon came to look upon the districts assigned to them as being virtually their own and to regard the native agriculturalists as their serfs."* The process of this evolution was facilitated by the fact that overlordship had long been one of the characteristic features of the Indian urban-centered empires, and furthermore, by *the incredible similarity between inland central Spain (Castile) and Latin America,* not only in terms of social structure, *but also in terms of the pastoral character of Spain's arid plains* (*Meseta*), which in climate, crop possibilities, and pasturage was nearly identical to the arid plateaus of the inland uplands of Latin America.‡

---

* Which had to be used in the islands and coastlands.

† The Arabs face a similar problem today of integrating the nomads into a state structure. Where permanent settlements are absent, this is quite difficult.

‡ Even Argentina and Chile and Southern California resemble central Spain in climate and soil conditions. It was here, rather than in tropical

"Following this precedent of land tenure, a system of overlordship came into existence in Mexico wherever the Spaniards found a native people already settled on the land."[6] For wherever an urban-centered or budding urban-centered empire existed, it fitted exactly the prerequisites for the Spanish *encomienda* system of overlordship. *Where it did not, the Spaniards had to import such people from Africa or abandon plans of permanent settlement.**†

Florida, that the main Spanish settlements occurred. Of course, the empire areas were the largest and most populous areas of colonization originally because of the compatibility of the social structure, which was more important as a factor than the climate and soil conditions. Only later was a lowland-semi-feudal estate structure worked out in the tropical areas, and these then became areas of heavy colonization.

* A description of the African importation in the islands and lowlands will be taken up. See also the importation of Africans into the south of the United States.

† Chile, with its hunting peoples, imported Incas to be serfs!

12

THE GROWTH OF CLASS DISTINCTIONS IN THE EMERGING INDIAN EMPIRES

THE GROWTH OF THE INDIGENOUS INDIAN CLASS STRUCTURE

Before the time of the Spanish conquest, certain modifications had been introduced which were gradually destroying whatever equality had formerly existed in the distribution of Indian land and in the social organization that was based on it. "Before the arrival of the Spaniards, modifications were already reducing the importance of the Indian village as the classic landholding unit of the country and were creating a form of tenure that closely resembled the individual holdings of post-conquest days."[1]

"An early departure from the communal system, in which each family held and worked an assigned plot of the commons, was *the growth of estates with serf-like tenants attached to the soil.* On these estates cultivation was carried on by peasants who *could neither move from the land nor be removed from it.*"[2] They were bound to the soil, and in case of a transfer of the estate, the peasants went with the land upon which they lived.

113

"Conversely, they enjoyed rights of occupancy,* the terms of which were established by custom and respected by the proprietor or overlord,"[3] usually a military aristocrat, but sometimes actually a commercial gentleman. This situation is a typical serf-peasant situation, as opposed to clans or agricultural village peoples, who had ownership of their own land and could leave it if they chose to, though they hardly ever did.

For the use of the soil these enserfed peasants "paid a share of the crops to the landlord and rendered him certain personal services, such as supplying him with the wood and water required for his household. He, in turn, was responsible for their protection and welfare"[4] in the typical style of the military noble-serf-peasant relationship.

Writing in 1538, Cortes gives a description of the conditions under which the tenants lived on certain estates at that time: "Each of the laborers received a piece of land for cultivation and a place upon which he might build a hut; in return, he worked on the farm of the landlord. Some of the tenants were also required to provide, at stated times, articles such as homespun cloth, loads of wood and turkeys; others were obliged to attend the landlord when he traveled and to carry his burdens; others again, wove cloth, both to make up the tribute which the landlord had to pay to the emperor and for the use of his household. The women also rendered personal service in the landlord's household."[5]

"So faithfully, indeed, has custom maintained these

* Called serf-right in Europe.

services which the [Indian empire serf] *was bound to render, that this account, written four centuries ago, is an excellent description of the relations* existing today between patron and peon [1927] on almost any large property in Latin America."⁶

The Indian estates there referred to, and described by the Spaniards . . . were "said to have existed from very early times and to have remained in possession of certain families [charismatic military or priestly clans] from generation to generation."⁷ Indeed, this method of landholding appears to have been quite common.

"All the military nobles high and low (of which there were said to be at least 3,000 in Mexico alone) as well as other persons [merchant-gentry, bureaucrats] held such estates before the conquest, and many of them retained their holdings for some years thereafter."⁸

"Other estates were attached to public offices and constituted part of the pre-requisites enjoyed by the officials"⁹—this latter being typical of bureaucratic power extension and estate establishment in urban-centered empires. "Since, however, the offices usually passed from father to son," each office being treated as an artisan skill, *"even these latter holdings came, more or less permanently, into the possession of certain families."*¹⁰ Most of the lands thus held by the aristocracy was seized and occupied by the Spaniards.

A small merchant-gentry class had also arisen in the Indian empires. The private individuals (*otras particulares*) referred to as possessors of estates may have been of this class of persons. Cortes in 1538 speaks of those who "were also not a prince of the blood, but had only been a large landowner."[11] Cortes says that some of the citizens (*vecinos*) of villages, particularly near the city of Mexico,* held extensive parcels of land, even as much as 1,000 or 2,000 measures (possibly from 1,020 to 4,080 acres). The tenants on these lands *paid rent* and rendered services on the same basis as the serfs (*mayeques*). Thus a typical merchant-gentry extension from the cities had occurred as in other urban-centered empires.

We can see then that "at the time of the Spanish conquest the communal system of landholding was actually in the process of being submerged."[12]

Another phase of this modification of the older system is to be seen in the extensive overlordship of villages or groups of villages "which had become general in the ancient Kingdom of Texcoco"[13] and elsewhere in Latin America. *"Districts had been granted to the chiefs and nobles surrounding the King."*[14] The Spaniards called these overlordships *senorías,* for these districts bore a remarkable resemblance to the semi-feudal private empire areas of the military nobles surrounding the Spanish kingship which were called *senorías.* The Spaniards thought these districts so similar in structure and operation that they used the same name to identify them.

The list of the *senorías* of Texcoco has been preserved, showing about thirty in all, each of which consisted of a number of villages. "In the Kingdom of Mexico (as dis-

---

* We may assume this to be true near all the great capital cities.

tinguished from the federation of Mexico, Texcoco, and Tacuba) a similar system was in operation. In this case, districts comprising one or more villages were held by the military nobles to whom tribute was paid. The possessions, or fiefs, carried a certain jurisdiction over land and people and were heritable."[15]

In the years following the Spanish conquest some Indian nobles* continued to hold these ancestral estates. Others presented petitions to the king of Spain or his representatives claiming villages or groups of villages as holdings that were recognized as having been in the possession of their families.

An illustration of this latter may be found in the "petitions sent by Indian nobles to Charles V in 1532, in which they specify the villages they had held and the manner in which they had come by them."[16]

"So thoroughly, indeed, had the systems become rooted in the country that the Spaniards adopted it as the basis of their own distribution of the land,"[17] showing the incredible consonance between reconquest Moslem Spain's urban-centered empire and the Indian empires.† *"The conquerors merely replaced the fallen Indian nobility and gentry and continued to receive from the inhabitants of the towns the tribute, labor, and other personal services that had been rendered to their aboriginal predecessors."*[18]

---

* Especially from Mexico and the Peruvian area
† Technological differences existed, of course, but the social structure, though less developed in America, was still similar.

LAND USAGE AND TRIBUTE STRUCTURE OF VILLAGES INCORPORATED IN INDIAN EMPIRES

The lands were distributed and held originally by clans and joint clan groupings (called *Calpulli* by the Mexican Indians, *Marca* by the Aymara Indians) living in the same settlement.*

The lands held by the joint-residence clan group of a village were of several kinds. In the first place "there was an area surrounding each village that was called the town land (in Mexico *altepetlali*). This seems to have included all the lands of various kinds that were held by the various kinship groups constituting the settlement. It was divided into sections, each (clan) holding its own well-defined part of this general area and using it independently of the other clans in the town."[19] Lands were also divided according to individual households within the clan units, and were often marked off and worked separately rather than communally except during harvest season.

In addition to the plots of land which were assigned to the clans, "fields were set aside for special public purposes, such as the production of supplies for the maintenance of the local noble, for the entertainment of official visitors, for the payment of tribute to the higher nobles,

---

* Typical of all late agricultural peoples. The Teutons used the same word to designate the groups of closely related clans (*Mark*) as the Aymara Indians (*Marca*).

for the prosecution of wars, and for the support of religious institutions and the priesthood."[20]

"The most important of these public plots were those *cultivated for the kings* and called in Mexico *tlatocatlalli,* (lands of the King).* *These were to be found in every village and were naturally the best lands.*†[21]

One can see, then, that a very typical kind of tribute, class-stratified arrangement for urban-centered empires was already in existence in Latin America, and that the diversion of tribute and services to the new conquerors could be culturally absorbed in such a social context much more readily than in a hunting or subsistence agricultural one. *What could be more consonant with the demands to be made by the Spaniards than such a structure—or more foreign to the hunting peoples?*

MODIFICATIONS INTRODUCED BY THE SPANIARDS

The Institutionalization of Semi-Feudalism in the Aboriginal Urban-Centered Empires

We have tried to show how the Indian empires were somewhat consonant with the Moslem empire, and that therefore the introduction of a social structure based upon the conquest of that empire would fit nicely upon the base of the Indian empires. We have also shown how this

---

* Called *mycwm lmmdo* in Europe.
† See Bandelier, *An Archaeological Reconnaissance into Mexico,* for details.

social structure could not fit on a base of hunting people on the tropical coasts, although it was re-created anyway through the importation of peoples upon whom it could be based.

However, it should also be remembered that, although the Spaniards based their reconquest social structure upon the Moslem empire, the final social structure of Spain was derived from a fusion of urban-centered characteristics derived from the Moslem empire with characteristics derived from French feudalism and, of course, the peculiar necessities of the particular circumstances in which it occurred.

The resulting social structure, which I have called semi-feudal, actually resulted in a vast alteration of the Moslem empire into something uniquely Spanish. This same Spanish alteration was accomplished in Latin America, and transformed the Indian empires into something similar to that which had occurred in reconquest Spain.

We turn now to the alterations of the Indian empires which the Spaniards accomplished, and their ramifications.

THE RAPID ALTERATION OF THE COMMUNAL LANDHOLDING SYSTEM BY THE SPANIARDS

Clan-communal landholding village patterns had not been fully eroded by the emerging class structure of the Indian empires at the time of the Spanish arrival. But under Spanish domination this ancient land system was thoroughly altered (except in the highest highlands and mountainous areas which the Spaniards could not use or could not survive in).*

"The struggle already begun between communal land-holding villages and large, private, [semi-] feudal estates was heightened and accelerated."[22] The Spaniards finished the job which the Indian upper classes had begun, and furthermore (1) destroyed the communal land-holding structure much more *completely* than the Indian empires would have,† and (2) destroyed the communal landholding system much more quickly than it would otherwise have been destroyed. These two alterations in the pace of direction of the social process had important ramifications for the emerging Latin American social structure.

Let us review for a moment the Indian empire social structure as it stood when the Spaniards took it, and then detail the changes which the Spaniards introduced into it in their attempt to consolidate their newly won lands with their own land distribution and utilization system.

LAND USAGE IN PRE-SPANISH INDIAN EMPIRES

"Before the coming of the Spaniards the population in the productive areas was organized in 'tribes.' Each tribe

* See altitude problem and Indian physical adaptation. (Larger lung capacity and higher hemoglobin count.)

† Semi-feudal, as compared to urban centered tribute empires, were historically much more destructive of agricultural village-communal land systems; see China and Southeast Asia, for example, in their 19th-century semi-feudal phase as compared to their empire phase.

was made up of a number of smaller units, which were kinship groups, or clans. The households composing the kinship groupings were settled closely together; and several distinct clans were generally grouped together in a village."[23] Bandelier states that the word *calpulli** was also used to designate a great hall or house, and we may therefore infer that, originally at least, all the members of one kinship unit dwelt under one common roof, or compound.[24] This is typical, the clan house originally housing all clan members in the early agricultural period.

"The Spaniards usually translated *calpulli* by the word *barrio* signifying 'district' or 'ward.' Without question the *calpulli* were primarily kinship groupings, but the organization of these units seems to have been modified in character through the settlement of the Indians upon the land as sedentary agriculturalists."[25] What originally had been kinship groups later on became place units, *"the land that was occupied tending to supersede blood relationships as the bond of union."*[26]†

As we have stated, then, originally the lands were communally held in double, triple, or larger, groups of clan holdings joined in a permanent village settlement.

---

* Joint clan group.

† This kind of land, rather than kinship, bond is part of the elective affinities of the serf-peasant class. Beginning in the late agricultural period, these affinities extend through the empire period and into the feudal or semi-feudal period (whenever these occur), and is broken only by the land alienation and money-commercialization pattern of early industrialism. Precisely this latter process is going on now in Latin America and the underdeveloped world generally: that is, the breakdown of serf-peasant elective affinities and land relationships, and their replacement with money-commercial land usage.

"There were grazing lands communally shared by the cluster of clans united in a given village, agricultural lands thus shared as well, and also private family lands heritable by clan."[27]

This village clan-cluster communal system was then altered by the emergence of the Indian empires.

First, crop surpluses only were demanded by the military and priestly and kingly upper strata, but slowly the land itself was taken by the upper strata as private estate lands, alienated from the peasant clans, with the peasantry itself reduced to tenantry, serfdom, and slavery.

Yet at the point of the Spanish arrival, the form of tenantry and serfdom was typical of urban-centered empires everywhere in that the peasantry, reduced to a negatively privileged class forced to give up surpluses of people, food, labor, and artisan production, still remained by and large in the village clan-cluster settlements, and still clung to the serf-right title to the land.

This at least gave them the security of their right to remain and work *their* lands as their ancestors had, thus preserving at least the crucial portion of the agricultural tradition. Moreover, it kept them at least partially, and often fully, within the reified authority structure of the empire, because they could grant *legitimacy* to the claims of the kingship and the aristocratic clans from the security of their own clan system which recognized the clan charismatic qualities asserted by the kingly and other aristocratic upper classes.

That is, paying deference, and even delivering tribute to, certain large, powerful, and therefore charismatized

clans was well within the traditional legitimacy structure
of the late agricultural period, and therefore even the
excesses that this situation took in the early urban-centered empire period could be borne by the clan-centered
peasantry—*as long as they remained clan-centered*—for
this was part of the tradition of the clans, though that
tradition had been extended almost to the breaking point
by the clan-charismatized upper strata.*

The breaking point of the legitimation given to the
kingship and positively privileged aristocratic clans by the
clan-village peasantry was just beginning to emerge as the
Spaniards arrived,† but had not yet emerged.

It remained for the Spaniards to inaugurate the full
destruction of the communal-clan-village landholding system and rip the peasant from his traditional place of
security, destroying the last vestiges of the legitimacy of
the overlordship of the positively privileged upper classes,
and throwing the now serf-slave peasantry into a permanent situation of partial anarchy, dereification from

---

* The Chinese, Southeast Asians, and Japanese peasantry remained in
their clan structure up until the twentieth century, until the clan-
charismatic authority of the kingships was broken by *outside* powers.
This kind of legitimacy and authority was broken early in Europe by the
Romans and by the decay of the Roman empire, and by the plague
where the village clan structure was shattered completely. The true-feudal
fief-manorial land relationship replaced clan and kinship relationships. As
we shall see, this is what occurred—though not as successfully in terms of
authority or legitimacy—in Latin America when the Spaniards replaced
the clan-charismatic empire legitimacy pattern with their semi-feudal
one.

† The picture was complicated by tribal conquests and poorly integrated outlying agriculturalists.

legitimate authority, and anomic disengagement from their clan ownership or serf-right to the land. The semi-feudal land system created by the Spaniards produced similar results in Latin America as it had in reconquest Spain, but without the Spanish kingship to re-unite, re-legitimate, and re-reify the populations living within it.

Summary of Land Usage Under the Indian Empires

(1) "In cultivation of the land, one portion dedicated to religious uses was given precedence . . . all joined in the planting and reaping of these crops."*

(2) "This and the similar service rendered on the (kingly) land, seems to have constituted the principle taxation imposed by the king of kings upon his people."[28] Though military service, household labor, concubinage, and human sacrifice were also demanded.

(3) After the preparation of lands set aside for the theocratically fused kings and priests, "that of widows, the infirm, and the wives of soldiers on duty was cultivated in the same manner."[29]

---

* The priests were the first positively privileged class, and priestly religious shrine areas preceded even the kingly cities in the growth of all "civilization."

(4) Finally "the land of the nobles (the military clan heads, a positively privileged stratum in an era of constantly threatening warfare) . . . was cultivated, all joining in the task."[30] Later, the land of the nonmilitary gentry was worked in the same manner, titles from the kingship at least partially legitimating these nonmilitary nobles.

All of this tribute farming that took priority over the subsistence the peasants engaged in for survival, occurred within the still existing security and legitimacy which the village-clan structure provided.

13

MODIFICATIONS INTRODUCED BY
THE SPANIARDS

As we have suggested, "though during the growth of the Inca, Aztec, and other Empires some modifications were introduced, it would appear that *the basis of the land system (the clan-village structure) remained almost unaltered* until the advent of the (Spaniards)."[1]

The land hunger of the Spanish conquerors caused many of the communities to disappear and brought about certain changes in those that remained, though the Spanish crown decreed numerous measures for the protection of the Indians and their land in its attempt to forestall the full growth of landed lords and private empires which would threaten its monopoly power position in the New World just as they had once done in the Old.*

* The Spanish kingship tried to protect the Spanish towns and peasants from semi-feudal excesses, but whereas they partially succeeded in this in Spain, they never succeeded in Latin America, for it was politically too distant, and the kingship was economically too dependent upon the mining and agricultural production which fostered the very conditions it was trying to prevent.

THE TRANSFORMATION OF COMMUNAL TRIBUTE VILLAGES INTO SEMI-FEUDAL MANORIAL CONDITIONS

As we have seen, most of the *encomiendas* consisted of villages or groups of villages in which the aborigines continued to hold their lands in common subject to the grant made by the Spanish crown, very much as they had under the Indian empires. But, "the gradual change of character suffered by the larger unit carried with it a modification of the smaller, and *the Indians passed from the status of free* [though tribute-bound to the Indian kingships] *communal landholders to that of serfs, bound more or less strictly to the estate upon which they lived*,"[2] and under the authority not of the clan headmen (*caciques*) but of the estate lords.

The Spaniards quickly transformed the communal tribute villages into semi-feudal private estates by (a) converting the villagers on the land grants into tenants who paid tribute (through labor and produce) directly to the estate owner; (b) through the elimination of the clan headmen and chiefs of the villages and their replacement with, or subordination to, the (1) foreman or overseer of labor on the estate, (2) the local Spanish bureaucratic official, and (3) of course, the estate lord himself.

It is not that the *cacique* did not often remain powerful, or *become* the foreman or local official, but that the *cacique* now gained his power through identification with the estate lord or Spanish crown, not through his clan affiliations. In fact, the *cacique* usually was not successful in transferring his position to his clan heir, but instead this position usually went to either (a) a mestizo—son of the lord by an Indian mother, or (b) an Indian who had learned to speak Spanish, learned the Spanish ways or skills, or had been politically useful to the Spaniards and thus was rewarded, or (c) to an Indian who had served in the army of the Spaniards, had done well, had learned the Spaniards' warfare techniques, and was rewarded by the Spaniards, or partly because he was held in awe by his own people.

Because of military conquest, disease, and dislocation (military service, mining, concubinage, and labor of other kinds), the remaining residents of depopulated villages fled to the safety of the semi-feudal manor and accepted its protective conditions, thereby giving up their claim to their lands and clan authority. The best lands were taken by the Spaniards; thus the Indians had a choice of poor lands and freedom, or good lands and serfdom.

(1) Military conquest: the blatant destruction of villages forced those left alive to flee to a nearby manorial estate for protection—they were thus absorbed* and incorporated there, losing their land and their clan associations.

(2) Disease: the infliction of European diseases upon the nonimmune Indians (small pox, scarlet fever, etc.) caused

* As in reconquest Spain and early feudal Europe.

depopulation and dislocation. Those remaining alive sought the refuge of the private estates and lost their lands and their clans in the chaos.

(3) Dislocation:

(a) Men were taken for military service and never returned, leaving some clans and villages unable to subsist alone—those remaining having either to enserf themselves totally or partially on the nearest estate.

(b) Mining: because of their need for a medium of exchange and raw materials for barter, the Spaniards accelerated mining operations far beyond those that the Incas or any of the other empire Indians ever had. Large numbers of men were removed from the villages as mine slaves. Though the Indian kings had done this, they never did it to the extent that villages and clans lost their ability to subsist, yet the Spaniards did this by accelerating and expanding their operations beyond the technological population density level of the Indian villages. The results were the same as the disease and military depopulations— that is, nonsubsisting villagers fled to and were incorporated into the *encomienda* private estates.

(c) Labor of other kinds, plus concubinage,* caused clans to fail to reproduce themselves sufficiently. And again, those remaining, plus those taken for labor and concubinage, ended up on the manorial estates of the conquerors.

---

* Also on a scale beyond that previously known, since the Spaniards had no women of their own to draw on, and had to rely completely on conquered peoples.

Thus, though the Indian empires were somewhat consonant with the Moslem empire, the Spaniards altered the urban-centered empire situation to that of semi-feudal private estate holdings, separated from the capital cities, just as they had done in Spain with the Moslem empire.

Spanish Modifications in the Indian Clan-Village Structure: Incorporation into the Spanish Authority System

While today's Indian village is the direct successor of the ancient Indian empire villages, one important modification was introduced into its organization as the result of the Spanish conquest: *The kinship bond which was the basis of the Indian village has almost, if not entirely, disappeared.*

It has been pointed out that even before the Spanish conquest, the clan cluster of communal land was becoming a place unit. The village, rather than the clan cluster, was gaining a reified* reality position. This change was accelerated by the confusion that resulted from the presence of the Spaniards and from the system of enforced service.

The introduction of foreign diseases and the great epidemics which followed also aided in the destruction of the ancient order . . . many clan-cluster villages were thus completely exterminated, while the Indians who survived were often scattered far from their original homes, and

* The village as a *social fact* was superseding the clan. The movement was from communal peasant to serf-elective affinities.

usually ended up enserfing themselves for land, food, and security.

Where it remained intact, the Indian village has always been obstinate in its adhesion to the collective method of tenure and in its resistance to private encroachments and to later official attempts to break up this time-honored system of the aborigines. The chaotic conditions prevailing in the early period of the Spanish conquest produced the destruction and transformation of these villages and the incorporation of their clan-bound inhabitants into the semi-feudal manor as negatively privileged clanless serfs, bound only to the land of the manor and under the civic and military authority only of the landlord.*

"There was a constant tendency to absorb whole villages into the great estates or to consolidate their fragments to form a modern rancho. Just as in earlier times (during the Indian empires' consolidations) some of the individual towns became, first tribute districts, then serf-lord estates; so after the conquest, the *encomiendas* were gradually transformed into private holdings tenanted by serfs."[3]

Furthermore, "many estates extended their bounds, by fair means or foul, to include neighboring agricultural villages. More frequently still, *the estate acquired the lands of the villages leaving their former holders to live as before but employing them as hired laborers, more or less*

---

* Or under priestly control and authority, since priestly authority was similar to other landed authority in Latin America. (Discussed in Chapter 17.)

in subjugation to the landowner. Thus the communal holdings gradually decreased in extent,"[4] banished to the poorest lands and the highest highlands where the Caucasians could not live. . . .* The Indians remained on the estates with certain rights of occupancy, recognized by the European custom, and in conformity with the mutual interests of landlord and peasant, but *"the ownership of the land was now vested in the conquering people."*[5] The Indian agriculturalists still had serf-right to the land—that is, the right to work it, no matter what lord owned it—but now in the feudal manorial sense rather than in the communal clan-village sense: that is, it wasn't *their* land that they had a right to work, but the land of the estate owner—he couln't throw them off of it, but it wasn't theirs . . .

Upon semi-feudal estates which had been formed by other than *encomienda* grants (usually through land extension of a *caballería*) serfs were also to be found, their presence being explained by the absorption of their lands into the estate, the occupants remaining as tenants upon the estate.

In other instances the natives, having lost the lands formerly cultivated in common, had been obliged to seek permission to settle upon the holdings of Spaniards. Under these conditions they received, as part of the wage for labor which they contributed to the estate, *"a hut (or*

* In Southeast Asia and Africa a similar pattern was formed.

the right to build one) and *a small plot of ground which they might work for themselves.*"[6]

One may see, then, that typical manorial conditions were reproduced on these estates—that is, serf-huts and serf plots could be found near the "great house" fortress and palace residence of the lord.*

Thus instead of a *village* settlement of clan-associated agriculturists communally farming their clan lands and paying tribute in terms of produce and direct labor to the "protecting" military nobles, we find a nonvillage settlement of serf-huts, with nonclan associated agriculturists having as their only bond their subordination to the lord of the estate in terms of military, civic, and religious jurisdictions. *Villages and clan relationships rapidly gave way to typical lord-serf relationships, and this became the standard pattern of relationships throughout most of Latin America* (though not in the highlands, mountains, and desert lands where the communal clan-cluster villages still remain to this day; but they are outside Latin American life, as it were, having never been—though their day is approaching—integrated into the body politic). "Master and man," "patron and peon," knight and squire . . . lord and serf, this is the pattern of relationship that allows one to understand the relation of the superordinate and subordinate classes in the Latin American countryside.

---

* This is quite similar to the process that went on in post-Charlemagne Europe, where the manors and castles were originally created after the chaos and insecurity of the dissolution of the Roman empire had destroyed the last vestiges of the European clan-village structure.

THE ESTABLISHMENT OF SERF-RIGHT BY THE DISPLACED INDIANS

"Prolonged residence on their allotted plot, and on the estate lands, coupled with generations of uninterrupted use, established a claim in the minds of the Indians."[7] Derived from the pre-Spanish nonalienable, clan-holding land and usage tradition of the Indians, and consonant with the Spanish semi-feudal notions of serf-right, the Indians developed certain subordinate rights of land usage on the Latin American semi-feudal estates.

In this and various other ways, these "subordinate rights grew up, established, and hedged about by custom" —"which defined more or less clearly the relations of lord and serf."[8] *

THE CIVIC REORGANIZATION OF THE VILLAGES

The Extension of Spanish Overlordship On† and Beyond the Estates

The civic organization, *which in the Indian villages had been based upon kinship,* did not long survive the con-

---

* As we shall see, certain problems concerning land usage and possession were never solved, though the system did operate fairly well for centuries.

† Many estates held whole villages intact as tenants.

quest. The clan heads, headmen, and *chiefs* (*caciques*)*
who acted as links to the kingship in the empires' tribute
system were gradually replaced by individuals who owed
their appointment either to the *encomenderos* or to the
Spanish crown officials.

Mayors, loyal to the Spanish kingly state, replaced the
caciques, or headmen loyal to their clans and to the
former Indian kingships. The mayors acted for the colonial government.

The "mayor" (*alcalde*), who took the place of the
headmen (*caciques*) as the head of the communal unit,
received his appointment from the local bureaucratic representative of the colonial government (*corregidor*), but
(and this shows the resiliency of the village organization
where it was left intact) "often in accordance with sug-
gestions of the Indians themselves."[9] In fact the *caciques*
actually maintain their power in outlying districts to this
day.

A church was also attached to each district, if not to
each village, and usually a priest was attached to each
estate. Thus, the priesthood acted as an extension of
Spanish authority over the Indian villages and manorial
serfs in the countryside.

Wherever the land was good, but communal villages
still remained intact, the Spaniards extended their authority over them by (1) introducing a local bureaucratic
official (*corregidor*) to collect taxes and carry out other

---

* See also the *Calpriquis* who were bureaucratic local functionaries
who linked the *caciques* to the Indian kingly states, collecting tribute,
etc.

tasks necessary to the central colonial government, (2) placing an official (*alcalde,* or mayor) loyal to the government to administer the village directly in place of the clan-cluster headmen, and (3) though barely mentioned, usually by placing a priest in or near the village to oversee religious affairs and to tie the Indians into the regional, national, and Spanish-empire hierarchical religious as well as civil structure.

The authority of the chiefs or *caciques* was thus undermined, if not destroyed.

The kinship groups were disrupted. Apparently the clan and the clan names have disappeared entirely in the more centrally located villages on the more desirable lands. Yet it is still possible to find vestiges of these kinship terms in local village organizations. They still exist fully in certain of the more remote villages. For example, "In Peru and Bolivia especially, there are still vestiges of the ancient lines that divided villages into different family groups."[10]

"The modifications introduced into the organization of the Indian villages by Spanish legislation, by the gradual breaking up of the kinship groups, by the progressive mingling of the two races* *brought about a close resemblance between the Indian villages and the towns which the Spaniards had founded.*"[11] In regions where the aboriginal influence was strong the Indian features prevailed, while in districts settled after the conquest by Spaniards or mestizos the characteristics of the Spanish towns were better preserved.

* The role of the mestizo is discussed in Chapter 18.

The distribution of these still surviving communities is determined largely by certain *geographical factors*: location, chiefly with respect to the travel routes, depth and character of the soil, and climatic conditions. Upon the colder heights and wind-swept, high plateaus the Indians were usually allowed to retain their lands and their clan-village social organization, but under different conditions, since they were *now cut off from the previously interdependent, centrally organized empire structure they had once been part of.*

Though the peasant villagers had been the lowest strata of these empires, and had to *give up* men, women, and produce, yet they had also *received* artisan products, variations in food products, and shared in the cultural as well as material expansion of the empires to which they were bound in tribute.

But after the Spanish conquest, the remaining peasant villagers found themselves (a) pushed off the best agricultural and grazing lands, and (b) cut off from the artisan production of the previous Indian empire cities. Pushed out and cut off, these Indian communities sank into a terrible poverty based on bare subsistence agriculture,* political isolation, and military vulnerability. Cast back, as it were, into the isolation of the once known past of the early agricultural period, but now existing not within the primeval natural setting of that epoch, but as a negatively privileged class on the fringe of a semi-feudal private empire world.

* They were often dependent upon estate wages when crops failed.

14

CONSEQUENCES OF THE CONVERSION FROM COMMUNAL TO SEMI-FEUDAL LAND CONTROL: THE CREATION OF PARTIAL ANARCHY AND ANOMIE

The centralized military and political systems, which the empires had struggled so long to create, were destroyed by the Spaniards. No military threat existed in Latin America after the Spaniards had conquered the entire territory. Therefore, the necessity for a unified military and political structure was removed. The continental and regional tribute systems were broken down into local fief systems. Central military alliances disintegrated, becoming unnecessary with the total Spanish military domination. The central reified authority structures were destroyed and replaced by the Spanish kingship, then slowly the authority of the Spanish kingship was replaced by exclusive local manorial control. This process left Latin America without any centralized reified authority structures beyond the walls of the private estates.

The centralized military-economic tribute systems of the Indian empires became disorganized after the Spanish conquerors took them over. The Spaniards tended to parcel out the lands of the Indian lords into private localized nonvassalized, nontribute, linked semi-feudal estates, as they had in reconquest Spain, rather than keeping the empire intact and ruling through its indigenous rulers as the Romans and Turks and English and others had done in their empires.

Though the Spanish kingship attempted to set up centralized military districts superimposed upon those of the Indian empires (the viceroyalty districts of Mexico and Peru corresponding closely to the jurisdictional districts of the Indian empires they had conquered), this attempt was not really successful.* The Indian empires' carefully arranged authority and alliance system soon disintegrated in the face of the feudally oriented conquerors despite the Spanish kingship's attempts to preserve the centralized empire structures for the purpose of establishing its own power on the new continent. The systems of surrogate kingship superimposed upon the empire districts,† called viceroyalties or governorships, rapidly declined in actual power, though these officeholders remained in an honorific capacity for two hundred years, until the wars of independence signaled the actual physical removal of the institution.

The Spanish colonists rapidly created their decentralized private empires. Fearing no military threat, having

---

* The kingship's attempt to maintain its authority is discussed in Chapter 16.
† To be discussed in Chapters 20 and 21.

decisively and totally destroyed the power of all the feuding empire and tribal adversaries, and following the traditional pattern which had grown up in reconquest Spain, the Spanish colonists created no vassalage-linked centralized political or military structure to replace the centralized Indian empires or alliances previously existing.

The Spanish lords had learned from the Inquisition in Spain that any centralized authority might act to curtail their private power. In fact, the Spanish centralized authority *was*, right at that moment, trying to limit their power.* *So the entire thrust of Spanish colonization was against centralizing authority and toward local fief control.*

This continued even after independence, the colonists always attempting to weaken rather than strengthen the central governments, and always dividing up the continent into lots of small countries rather than leaving the land divided into the larger units of vast viceroyal districts corresponding to the vast Indian empires.

Thus, instead of replacing the Aztec, Inca, and other Indian empires' trend toward centralization and unifying authority structures, the Spanish conquerors—against the will of the Spanish centralized kingship—initiated a trend toward diffusion of power to the individual semi-feudal estates and the local areas of private ownership and control. This left Spanish America in semianarchy, with no

---

* See Chapter 16, on the new "Laws of the Indies," promulgated by the Spanish centralized state, which attempted to block estate formation as a heritable right.

clan-village or tribal interlocking territorial controls, and no centralized, militarily dominant aristocratic vassalage alliances. Therefore, though local lords had full control of their individual estates, between these private holdings, total anarchy reigned . . . just as in reconquest Spain.*

Along with the centralized military and political system, the centralized economic system of the empires was destroyed. The well-organized system of artisan and agriculture production and distribution broke down. Agricultural and artisan goods were *imported*, not produced internally, because the great quantities of precious metals being shipped to Spain could be used as easy barter for all staple and luxury items necessary for the support of life on the new continent. Thus the production of raw materials as barter for consumption goods replaced internal productive organization in Latin America as early as the sixteenth century!

Labor usage was limited almost exclusively to manorial usage. The great projects (temples, etc.) of the Indian empires vanished in favor of the smaller scale of more typically feudal projects, such as churches. However, city-building, though on less grand a scale than that of the Indian empires, did occur, and mining, of course, was increased a hundredfold.

But even this centrally directed labor usage soon gave way to more localized labor usage, and the carefully controlled slave-labor projects of the Indians' capital cities were eventually replaced with the more haphazard usage

---

* Pre-Shogun Japan was a remarkably similar case as was warlord China and Southeast Asia in the late nineteenth century.

of dislocated shack-dwellers, living around the emerging Latin American cities, as low-wage seasonal laborers.

The social system of the Indian empires was also significantly altered by the Spaniards. Clan, village, and tribal ties were broken and replaced with feudal-manorial ties. But the transition was too brutal and too rapid for the new legitimacy and authority systems to take hold completely.

Arising from this, a large dislocated class of Indians was created that was never integrated into the manors. They were only peripherally involved in the social structure in terms of mining, seasonal harvest labor on the estates, and occasional city-building and projects in general.

THE AMBIGUOUS STATUS OF THE MESTIZO

Also, as a partial concomitant to the social reorganization that accompanied land reorganization, there was the utilization of Indian women as sexual slaves, companions, and concubines; and also as wives, where Spaniards married into wealthy, landholding clans. As a result of this, mestizos began to occur in large numbers. Remember that the Spaniards had no women with them in the early years of the conquest, nor was puritanism—just emerging in Europe—ever a force in Southern Europe.

Part neither of the Indian class system, nor of the Spanish overlordship, the mestizo found himself in a peculiar social position, and tended to drift in an anomalous status between the Indian village world in the hills and the Spanish estate world on the plains, swelling the ranks of the already existing class of dislocated Indians.

In most cases they rejected the negatively privileged status of the Indians and refused serfdom under any permanent conditions. They aspired to the Spanish lordly status, became aggressive at accumulating small property holdings with the intention, of course, of eventually creating an estate. But even the small holdings they could acquire were largely taken by Spanish foot soldiers and lesser military figures. In fact, since not all Spaniards were able to receive lands, the chances for the mestizo to receive land, and the definite status that went with it, were quite slim.

With the chance for land and Spanish status small indeed, and with their rejection of the subordinate Indian status, the mestizos began to drift and live an existence sanctioned by neither estate nor village mores. They became the main body of an anomic, unintegrated, dislocated class destined to swell to vast proportions, first with the political dislocations of the independence wars, then as the commercialization of the countryside proceeded in the nineteenth and early twentieth centuries.

They lived in semipermanent encampments in the hills between the highland villages and the plateau estates and worked as seasonally employed, but not enserfed, agricultural workers, paid in monetary wages, during the harvest season, then disappeared into the freedom of the hills once more. They provided temporary labor in the early cities, again for direct wages, but since there was no real industry as yet, they drifted away when their temporary services had been fulfilled and their wages spent on the pleasures of the city (for which they had come in the first place).

The lucky among them, usually relatives of the estate lord through the maternal line, became foremen and overseers on the semi-feudal estates. This group, too, existed midway in status and role between the Indian serfs and the Spanish overlords.

The unlucky among them, usually the very ambitious who had been thwarted in their attempts to gain status, became professional thieves and bandits inhabiting the trails between the cities and the estates or living in the labyrinths of the Latin American Andean hills; or they became roustabouts, drunks, and troublemakers inhabiting the cafés and brothels of the cities and living in shacks on the outskirts of the cities.

In this early period, however, this dislocated class of racially mixed individuals was neither large nor problematical, for the cities were still inconsequential frontier and port towns, and seasonal labor in the countryside was welcomed, although the mestizos' arrogant, nonserf, aggressive, disrespectful, unpredictable behavior was not.

A further alteration in the social structure that occurred was that the villages *not* incorporated into the semi-feudal estates were cut off from their previous empire ties and left as early agricultural enclaves, but on the worst land, so that agricultural production was drastically reduced. These villages lacked the artisan production previously gained through barter from the Indian capital cities and towns, and they also lacked tribal or empire military protection.

RAPID LAND ALIENATION AND THE SERF'S DREAM

On another level of analysis, the rapid alterations of the Latin American social structure by the Spaniards had consequences for the reality structure in which the Indians lived. For those Indians incorporated into the semifeudal estates as serfs, having been ripped out of their clan structure and wrenched off their village lands too quickly, always held, beneath their outwardly subservient exteriors, a longing for the return of their traditionally owned inalienable clan lands.

The alienation of land from clan and individual households created great hostility, instability, anomie, and feelings of dislocation in the newly enserfed Indian populations.

The alienation of the communally held village lands and their subsequent reorganization into semi-feudal estates, and the *total* enserfing of the Indians and their *total* loss of personal land and clan holdings was alien— *and remained alien*—to the Indian populations. For though "the innovations in the ancient land system introduced by the Aztecs and other conquerors was undermining this system, it had not yet destroyed it. The proportion of territory occupied by the tenanted estates was probably quite small as compared with that held by the village-clan groupings, while the tribute districts were only

beginning to take on the character of landed property."[1]
At the point of the Spanish conquest, *"the landholding village* certainly remained the dominant unit in the agrarian system"[2] of the just centralizing Indian empires. Now the restructuring of any late agricultural people into a class-divided, privilege-divided, urban-centered empire, with its concomitant land alienation from ancient clan ownership and conversion of a free peasantry into a bound serf-peasantry, could be expected to cause hostility and instability among those forced into a negatively privileged class situation *wherever it occurred.*

This process usually took centuries (as it surely would have in Latin America) and was cloaked in clan-charismatic and religious symbols that had a legitimizing effect on the total process. The Spaniards, however, accomplished this restructuring of land tenure and privilege in but a *few short years* due to their high stage of military prowess, previously unknown in the New World, and their centuries of experience in the restructuring of the Moslem empire.

Therefore, in effect, the Spaniards accomplished the transition to lord-serf, land-privilege relationships too quickly and too efficiently, and without the accompaniment of clan-charismatic and religious* symbols familiar to the Indian populations. Neither time nor a legitimating ideological structure could support or ameliorate the feel-

---

* The Indians found the Christian religious symbols confusing and inapplicable. Amusing stories are told of the Indians' inability to understand the trinity and the one-God idea together. Christianity otherwise acted as a partial legitimating institution.

ings of bewilderment and hostility engendered by the anomic, negatively privileged position in which the Indian populations found themselves.

Already accustomed to living under a reified, centralized authority structure, these Indian populations capitulated and allowed themselves to be enserfed, in contrast to those hunting and early agricultural peoples who did not. The latter kept fighting, were exterminated through forced slavery, or withdrew to the dense forests of the interior. But the loss of the clan landholdings occurred too quickly and was never legitimated; it always remained a source of contention and hostility. (As previously mentioned, most of the Indians had come from tribute villages which provided services and food to the centralized military-priestly authority, but which had maintained ownership of their clan village lands.)

This then, the *total* land alienation, which the Spaniards inaugurated with great vigor and greed (and accomplished in a remarkably short time), was the major important nonconsonant feature of the restructuring of the Indian social structure by the Spaniards. This dissonance of structure led to great difficulties, tensions, and uprisings amongst the peasants previously integrated into the Indian empires, for neither the public plots (tribute productive lands) nor the parcels assigned to clan households could be alienated *under any circumstances* under the Indian empires.* Not even the nobles or the emperor

---

* Land alienation in China and Southeast Asia generally took place on a rapid, grand scale, as in Latin America. In China, it occurred when the partly semi-feudal, partly imperial structure broke down under Western penetration.

might take them from the village clan-clusters,[3] though they had just begun to do so at the time of the conquest.

Yet, the Spanish overlords took all of the good lands almost immediately. This left an unresolved anger amongst the enserfed Indians, and created a messianic myth of some future redemption-in-land for the enserfed populations.

Rather than creating a legitimation for their land reorganization system, by their rapidity and violence the Spaniards created an antilegitimating myth of the eventual overturning of the new land system and a return to the old, and left a permanent legacy of anarchic hostility against the system which was to appear in various forms of naked force against the system, from banditry, to revolution, to quixotic caudilloism.

The cry of revolt in Latin America is always prefixed by "Land!"*

A Summary of the Consequences of the Conversion

Thus military, political, and economic localism grew up because:

(1) No military threat existed any more, with total Spanish domination and Spanish kingly armies sent from Spain and ready in any emergency.

(2) Political control was sought by the estate lords as completely private feudal control (with no vassalage links,

---

* The same cry is heard in other areas emerging from colonial domination: Russia, Slavic Europe, China, Southeast Asia, Africa, and the Middle East. It was also a factor in the English and French revolutions.

as in Spain), any centralizing attempt being viewed as a threat to their private power.

(3) Economic supplies—artisan and agricultural—were purchased from Europe (through Spain as the monopolistic middleman) in return for the abundant supplies of metals from the mines.

15

THE RE-CREATION OF THE SPANISH SOCIAL STRUCTURE WHERE THE INDIGENOUS STRUCTURE WAS NOT COMPATIBLE

Where urban-centered empires did *not* exist, as on the islands and in the tropical lowlands of Central and South America (especially the east coast and the Amazon valley of Brazil), the Iberians had great difficulty establishing a social structure along the lines they had learned in reconquest Spain. In fact, as we have mentioned, when they attempted to establish their semi-feudal social structure on the islands through the *encomienda* land-clan granting system they almost succeeded in wiping out the indigenous hunting and early agricultural peoples, and totally failed in their attempt at re-creating a semi-feudal estate structure.

But, after these initial failures followed the great successes of the Spaniards in re-creating the desired social structure upon the base for which it had been developed, that of urban-centered empires.

Flushed with their great success in Mexico and greater Peru (an area that now encompasses Peru, Bolivia, Para-

151

guay, North Chile, Ecuador, and parts of Colombia), the
Iberians began to realize that already enserfed or enslaved
peoples, or peoples acquainted with serfdom and slavery
as part of their everyday reality structure, would accept
the slave or serf status, whereas those unacquainted with
such a role and status in their reality system, would not.

The Iberians found that not only could they call upon
these enserfed Indians to continue their labor and tribute
under the new overlordship in their old territories, but
that they could move these Indian serfs from one area to
another, and they would still respond as serfs. Militarily
they would fight, as they always had, as foot soldiers under
the generalship of the aristocratic militarily specialized
clan heads. Economically, they would work the fields and
mines. They would act as personal servants in the household of the lord, as squire to the knight on the road, and
in battle they would give their sons as soldiers and laborers and priest's helpers and temple guardians, and their
daughters as concubines and wives. They did this for the
Spanish just as they always had for their Indian overlords.

THE ESTABLISHMENT OF SEMI-FEUDAL
ESTATES IN TEMPERATE NON-EMPIRE
AREAS

The new overlords, then, who had settled in areas where
no enserfed Indians existed, and who soon discovered that
the hunting peoples would not accept a negatively privileged status, began to *import* serfs from the great empires

and to use them to establish semi-feudal lord-serf estates where none had ever existed, where empires had never previously been founded.

The case of Chile is a perfect example. In Chile no enserfed Indians were to be found, for the Inca empire had not yet extended its tentacles that far south. The inhabitants of the Chilean temperate forests were hunting peoples like those in the similar climate and terrain of North America. These hunting peoples—the Araucanians —fought the Spaniards savagely and never stopped fighting.* Rather than accept a negatively privileged serf status, which to huntsmen was equivalent to loss of their warrior status, the hunting people withdrew farther and farther southward into the dense forests.

The Iberians never pacified or enserfed these huntsmen who continued to fight on until modern times, and though the Iberians took most of their land, they never could exact their labor, or tribute of any kind. Those prisoners who were taken remained uncooperative even when beaten severely, and usually died, either from brutality, punishment, or personal shame.†

However, during their seesaw battle with the Araucanians for the possession of their lands, at one point in the struggle, after a severe reverse when Valdivia himself was captured, tortured, and killed by the Araucanian in their first successful counteroffensive against the Spaniards, re-

---

* The Araucanians were divided into two tribes, one being totally wiped out by the Spaniards, the other fighting on until modern times.
† As did the United States Plains Indians.

inforcements in the form of Inca recruits were brought down from the highlands of Peru. When the fighting had ended successfully (though the Araucanians never stopped fighting but were driven deeper and deeper into the forests), the Spaniards did not return the Incas to their own lands, but retained them as serfs in Chile and created the typical semi-feudal estate pattern founded elsewhere on the Indian empire bases. A regular pattern of Inca importation then began in those areas south of the empires where no enserfable Indians existed. This pattern proved to be highly successful and the semi-feudal social structure based on *encomienda* grants now came to be re-created all over *temperate* South America, merely by including in the *encomienda* grant such and such an amount of serfs imported from the nearest Indian empire, usually after military campaigns had already brought these serfs under the control of a Spanish military overlord far from the site of the original village homeland of the soldiers in question.

As to women for the use of the overlords and the newly enserfed, dislocated empire Indian soldiers, either they were captured from the hunting tribes, which gave an added incentive to the newly recruited soldiers to fight hard for a needed prize, or in rarer cases were brought down from the Indian empires as concubines for the Spaniards and wives for the serfs.

The plunder of women was more common than the importation of empire women, as the hunting women, unlike the men, were already in a position of negatively privileged status within the rigidly sex-stratified hunting bands. Already dominated politically and exploited economically by the weapon-monopolizing men, already working from dawn to dusk on subsistence artisan and gathering tasks and the tending and curing of animal hides, the women, with an added culturally demanded response—that of glorifying and charismatizing the victors of war—responded positively to their new status as equal to or an *improvement* upon that previously held by them in the hunting band. Their work was often reduced; their quarters were better; their treatment by both the serfs and the lords was as good or better than by the hunters; and their traveling labors (especially during pregnancy) were cut down.

Therefore, the hunting women, in terms of acquiescence to subordination and in terms of little status alteration, accepted their serf status. Together with the importation of male serfs from Indian empires, this allowed for a situation permitting semi-feudal estates to be founded in Chile. Argentina and other temperate South American areas followed this example.*

THE ESTABLISHMENT OF SEMI-FEUDAL ESTATES IN TROPICAL AREAS

The system of importation of Indian serfs from empire areas which was working so well in the temperate and

* Argentina was barely populated, thus no serfs were imported, and later, Europeans came in to take up the open land. To Chile, too, they came, but less so because in Chile the land was taken with estates. In Argentina and also temperate South Brazil where fewer estates existed, more land was open to immigration.

highland areas did not, however, have any success in the
tropical and lowland areas, for it was rapidly discovered
that the Indians, for *physical* reasons, could not work in
the tropical lowlands. We now know—though the
Iberians did not know the reason—that the Indians had
developed a special blood and lung adaptation to the
rarified climate of the highlands; though they can survive
there better than any other people, they cannot survive
well in the heavy, humid, hot air of the lowlands where
conditions are reversed.

Therefore, when these empire Indians were imported to
the tropics (with great enthusiasm after the Chilean successes), they failed to respond as expected. They died of
disease, appeared lackadaisical, tired easily, collapsed, and
died from exhaustion. In general, they simply could not
work, and could barely survive.

The Portuguese in Brazil

The Iberians were at a loss as to what to do next and
almost abandoned the tropical areas. In fact, the Spaniards *were* abandoning the tropical lowlands and moving
steadily to the high plateaus and temperate climates. The
West Indies became like ghost towns, a graveyard for
hunting and empire Indians, a land of poverty and labor
for the Spaniards. But the Portuguese could not abandon
the lowlands, for almost their entire territory, that which
is now called Brazil, was lowland and tropical in its character. In Brazil, after futilely attempting to enserf the
hunting Indians and finally driving them deep into the in-

terior of the impenetrable Amazon jungle, and after the importation of conquered highland peoples failed, a new source of serf labor had to be found, or the entire colony would have had to be abandoned.

In Brazil a rudimentary estate structure had been created through the union of Portuguese men with captured or compliant hunting women and constant importation of captured serfs and slaves from among the inland agricultural Indians.* But the Indians had to be replaced continually because they died off: there simply were not enough agricultural Indians around for the establishment of a stable, reproducing serf population.†

But yet the system operated for a time in this fashion through a constant new supply of serfs and the union of Portuguese overlords with numerous captured concubines, so that the semi-feudal lord-serf estate system was firmly established as the permanent social structure in Brazil, even though it was in danger of not maintaining itself.

At this point, a short look at Portuguese history previous to its conquest of Brazil is necessary.[1]

Portugal, firstly, is the tropical lowland area of the

---

* The Indians of Brazil were actually agricultural in many areas, engaging in slash-and-burn agriculture. However, though these Indians made up the bulk of the early slave-serfs, their numbers were not great enough, and nothing like an empire had even been established. The population density of the area was always well held down by the Amazon jungle which grew so quickly and contained such pestilence as to reduce agricultural productions and the population potential.

† Serf-hunting—a sort of human pirating venture—was common in Brazil. Bands of Portuguese and mestizos would raid interior Indian villages and bring back a supply of serfs. But this was too slow a process and not nearly productive enough.

Iberian peninsula, and therefore the Portuguese were the best adapted among the conquering Iberians to such a climate. Secondly, under the Moslem empire—and continuing after the reconquest of Lusitania by the Portuguese—there were estates upon which Moslem-captured slaves and serfs had worked. Amongst these Moslem slaves had been some from the sub-Sahara lands of the Sudanese strip running east and west from coast to coast below the Sahara and above the jungles of the Congo valley.

These African slaves from the budding kingships of the Sudanese regions—and those captured by them from the peoples living to the south—impressed the Portuguese by their ability to work hard in and withstand the tropical climate, and by their willingness to do so. "He works like a Moor" was their saying[2] (this especially impressed the reconquest Portuguese with their antiwork ethic).

After the Moslems had been defeated, it was the Portuguese who first followed their trail into Africa, and it was the Portuguese who—first among Europeans—continued the Moslem practice of raiding and bartering with the African budding kingships to obtain slaves and serfs to keep their own plantations going (and later as marketable commodities for other peoples who desired slaves).

The Moslems had an international slave-trade system, from the Viking sale of captured Slavs (this is where the word slave came from in Anglo-Saxon—Slav became slave) in East and Southeast Europe, to the Southeast Asian islands, to the African Sudanese and jungle belts.

The Portuguese, for geographic reasons of proximity, raided the West African coast (the Moslems continued to control and raid the East African one until modern times), and established their permanent slave exportation centers on the Gold Coast, relying on water routes rather than land routes as the Moslems had. This was a piece of good luck for the Portuguese, since the Africans of the coastal rain forests were delighted to take the opportunity the Portuguese gave them for revenge against the Northern Sudanese and plains peoples who had been selling them into slavery to the Moslems for four centuries. Since the Moslem trade routes emanated north from the Sudan to the Mediterranean, the Sudanese had been raiding their southern neighbors to supply slaves as an exchange commodity for luxury goods and cloth from the Moslem empire. Now the southern peoples were able to reverse the process, raiding northward (with rival kingships and tribes raiding each other as well) for slaves to supply to the Portuguese. They carried out their task with a spirit of vengeance born of centuries of like treatment by the northerners and southern regional rivals, and the Portuguese slave trade prospered beyond their expectations.

Thus it was the Portuguese who, having already institutionalized the system of using Africans in their own tropical lowlands, hit upon the idea of importing them to Brazil and other tropical areas to act as serfs and slaves in order to maintain the semi-feudal estate structure in the tropical areas, and to establish it where it had not been maintained previously.

The Africans, as budding urban-centered empire peoples living under rudimentary kingly reified authority
structures (still reifying), and thus enserfable and enslav-
able, having lived for centuries under traditional slave-
captive conditions exacerbated and exploited by the
Moslems, then the Europeans, accepted their negatively
privileged serf and slave statuses just as the empire Indians had; and in the case of the Africans, women were
brought along with the men.

The Africans, already incorporated into the Moslem
empire, could function easily in the Spanish one with all
of its Moslem features.

This system was transplanted rapidly by the Portuguese
and Spaniards to all of the tropical islands and lowlands,
and the Iberian semi-feudal estate structure was thus
re-created where it had failed previously, a consonant base
being imported where none had existed.*

Observations on the Consonant Bases of Societies

The importation of peoples who then form a consonant
base—that is, carrying the elective affinities of the society
to be re-created—is a successful way, then, to establish a
society where the desired kind of society is alien to the
populations existing in a given area. The peoples "imported" do not have to be of the same nationality, but
merely of the same class as those in the society to be
copied, for coming from that same class, they will share

* The English later brought East Indians over for the same purpose.

similar elective affinities and social realities with those of the society trying to reproduce itself.

The example here is a case in point. Africans from a similar class, ideology, and social background as empire Indians and kingly Iberians were able to function well in the setting desired by the Iberians on the new continent. The north of the United States, Canada, Australia, and South Africa exemplify similar situations. Whether the immigrants be English, Dutch, French, or Scotch, Welsh, or Irish is unimportant. It is their class position, ideology, and reality that is the crucial factor.

Israel, though a modern example, can be used to illustrate the same point. When she imported a European middle class she easily established middle-class institutions, but when she imported a semi-feudal Jewish merchant class from North Africa and the Middle East, she failed to be able to integrate the first generation into her European institutions.

Another example is the United States' ease of integration of middle-class Jewish immigrants, contrasted with the failure to integrate Negroes from a southern plantation economy and Mexicans from semi-feudal estates, as well as the difficult integration of the Eastern and Southern European peasants (the Northern European immigrant peasants having been integrated as free farmers in America, a status they partially held in Northern Europe already).

"It is worth noting, also, that the development of industrial societies have frequently depended upon the existence or importation of classes that were amenable to industrial conditions of work."[3] The free movement of laboring classes from one industrial society to another was always seen as a more favorable process than the converting of an indigenous nonlaboring class into a laboring class (as in Australia and South Africa). Also, much of early industrialization depended upon cheap labor when capital was scarce. Therefore if cheap laboring classes were not indigenously available, they were often imported. Chinese were imported to build the United States railroads because United States labor was too expensive. German and Russian political prisoners were used to build the Russian railroads. East Indian laborers were imported in various parts of the world to provide the same function.

Of course, educational and social-work programs can alter a class of people so that they do become assimilable and mobile, but this was unknown as a political policy until the twentieth century, and is almost always a two to three generational process.

EARLY COMMERCIAL NATURE OF THE
LOWLAND ESTATES[4]

One difference existed between the highland estates and the lowland estates. From the beginning it was impossible to grow subsistence crops on a large scale in the tropics. The traditional Iberian staples plus the traditional Indian empire staples—wheat, corn, cattle, etc.—simply could not be maintained in the thin tropical soil with the heavy and constant rainfall and high temperatures. It was because subsistence agriculture was not possible that the areas were inhabited by hunting peoples almost exclusively in the first place.

Therefore, given the fact that practically all subsistence products could be bought through Spain in return for raw materials or rare products, these tropical estates began to turn to the growing of export crops instead of subsistence crops to be used to purchase subsistence as well as luxury items. *From the beginning* tropical fruit, sugar, kemp, cocoa, coffee, rubber, and other products were cultivated *commercially*, to be used as trade items.

Thus these estates never had a subsistence character, yet they maintained all the other characteristics of the semi-feudal estates—the lord-serf relationship and all that followed from it.

But this one difference, the immediate commercial character of the lowland estates, was quite crucial in that these areas subsequently avoided the period of difficult transition from subsistence to commercialized cash-crop estates which racked the highland and temperate areas for a century and a half after independence. This is what gives the history of Cuba, Puerto Rico, and Brazil the appearance of being less chaotic, less stormy, less blood-filled than the other Latin American states.* This fact,

---

* With the coming of the Portuguese kingship to Brazil during the Napoleonic era, instead of years of warfare, they had quiet and the presence of a centralized kingship; it should also be remembered that the Spanish kingship never lost control of Puerto Rico and Cuba until modern times (Spanish-American War).

which is often attributed to the Portuguese less *machismo*, more lackadaisical character or to a less rebellious attitude of the African and mulatto than the Indian and mestizo, actually derives from the two facts described above: first, the immediate cash crop-commercialization of the tropics creating no need for a period of commercial conflict with noncommercial landed estate-holders; and second, the calming, reifying presence of the Portuguese kingship in Brazil during the independence period, when Spanish America was involved in twenty years of constant military turmoil.

But when we arrive at the twentieth century, the differences in the histories and social structures of the tropical and temperate areas become minimal. As we shall see, the social structures of the entire Latin American area had become more similar than different—though variations occurred from country to country, of course, such as the European settlement in temperate areas altering the social structure somewhat in the nineteenth and twentieth centuries.

But we are getting far ahead of ourselves—the task *here* was to show that *the semi-feudal estate structure with its lord-serf relationships had been fully established, superimposed first upon the compatible Indian empire bases, then, where no compatible base existed,* upon a base of serfs imported to temperate areas where they could survive from the Indian empires in the north, and second, upon the African kingly tribal groupings just emerging as urban-centered empires (or incorporated into the Moslem one) imported to the tropical areas where the empire Indians could not survive and the male hunting Indians would not accept such a negatively privileged status.

16

THE TRIUMPH OF SEMI-FEUDALISM
ON THE NEW CONTINENT

THE RE-ESTABLISHMENT OF LORDLY
CONTROL WITHOUT THE KINGSHIP

As first understood in the West Indies, the *encomienda* was a temporary concession to be surrendered at the will of the crown for the kingship knew from previous experience in Spain that a permanent hereditary serf-military landed class would constitute a barrier to its authority, and thus tried to prevent the permanent establishment of such a social structure.

Therefore, "as the system became established the term of possession was defined as 'one life,' that is, to last during the life of the recipient. By 1536 the term had been extended to include 'two lives,' that of the holder and that of his heir. It was made still more permanent in 1629 by the addition of a third life, and later, under certain conditions, a fourth and a fifth were added."[1]

"The encomienda thus came to be regarded as the actual possession of the families which held them, being virtually hereditary."[2]

THE SPANISH KINGLY STATE ATTEMPTS TO PREVENT THE LORDLY AND PRIESTLY LAND CONTROL

The Abolition of the "Encomiendas"

The Spanish kingship attempted to block the growth of the lordly and priestly landed class and maintain its monopoly as middleman controller on all trade and produce coming from and going to the new territory (and also to protect its direct source of revenue from the crown-owned lands).

To this end the kingship in 1542 passed the "New Laws of the Indies" which "provided for *the total abolition of the encomiendas* and for the complete reform of colonial administration in America."[3]

The abolition of the *encomiendas* was intended to begin the dismemberment of these large holdings, with the idea of repeating the successful performance by the kingship that it had carried off in Spain—that is the reduction of the lordly and priestly landed class, and the usurping of all military, economic, political, and religious power into the centralized, bureaucratized kingly state. However, such a conclusion was not to occur in Latin America. The drama began in the same manner, but when the curtain dropped a new cast was to take a bow.

In spite of the king's efforts, the permanence of the *encomienda* grants was already assumed by the colonists.

This became apparent when the new laws* of 1542, which had provided for the total abolition of the *encomiendas* and for the complete reform of colonial administration in America, met with such stormy opposition in Mexico and Peru, the two main areas of early colonization situated over the two great Indian empires, that it was necessary to repeal them.

Repeated attempts by the kings to protect the serfs and inhibit the power of the lords were of no avail. "The colonies were far too distant, the local authorities too much in sympathy with their settlers' needs," for they were often consonant with their own, "and there was no substitute for the labor of the natives . . ."⁴

The kingship fought this institutional trend at every turn, delayed it as long as possible, "but overextended militarily in Italy and on the European continent, and totally dependent upon wealth produced in Spanish America, it failed utterly in its attempts to retain its authority in Spanish America"⁵ and prevent the growth of private, clan-charismatic semi-feudal lordly empires.

REASONS FOR THE FAILURE OF THE KINGSHIP IN THE NEW WORLD

(1) ECONOMIC: In Spain, during the kingship's battle with the estate lords and priests, the kingship was economically dependent upon the town merchants who be-

---

* The "New Laws of the Indies."

came its major ally in its struggle to consolidate and centralize the military and political power of the realm.* However, in Latin America, the Spanish kingship was dependent upon the estate-lords and their serfs in terms of mining and agricultural produce! The estate lords held a trump card.

Thus, whereas in Spain the kingship's economic policy could act as a stranglehold on the noncommercial lordly and priestly class, in Latin America it was the lordly and priestly class that held the kingship in an economic noose. The economic strings in both cases worked to the success of the holder, and thus in Latin America the kingship found itself in the anomalous position of desiring the political eradication of a class which it was forced to encourage and protect economically. For if Spain were cut off from her economic resources in the New World she would collapse instantly. This is why she fought so long and so hard to hold onto her colonies, and this is why she *did* collapse instantly when her colonies diverted economic produce to England and France and then to the United States after independence.

Thus the total dependence of the kingship on mining, herding, and agricultural output from the new continent placed the kingship in a position where it could do nothing to interfere with the *productivity* of the new continent or else risk total economic disaster at home. Since the *encomenderos* and other estate- and serf-holders were the chief productive sources in the early colonial period,

* This was the typical alliance all over postfeudal Europe.

the kingship found it impossible to impose any political regulations upon them that would have interrupted production.

(2) MILITARY: Originally, the *conquistadores* themselves were the only military force in Latin America and they, of course, became the estate lords the kingship later sought to curb and control. Though it did eventually do so, it was some time before the kingship established its professional army in the New World under commands loyal only to itself.

But even after the establishment of the kingly professional army on the new continent, the vast territorial dispersal of the settlers made complete military surveillance impossible. It was also easy, before the wars of independence started military confrontations in earnest, for the lords and priests to buy off military commanders with promises of land and office and wealth in the New World.

One should also remember that Spain was rapidly expanding on the European continent as the new master of the Holy Roman Empire and therefore had vast troop commitments in Italy, the Low Countries, England, and even France for a time. The kingship had a Holy Roman Empire as well as a vast continent to police. It could not control Latin America while overextended in Europe. It was only after Napoleon pushed the Spanish army out of Europe—two centuries after the discovery—that Spain was able to turn its armed strength against its colonies in full force. Of course, it was then too late.

(3) POLITICAL: Economic power brought political power, and the indigenous estate owners, lordly and priestly, and city middlemen-merchants who made up the representatives of the regional parliaments convened in the capital cities* began to take over complete control of political matters. They even oversaw the doling out of *encomiendas*, first by the grace of the king but then by the "grace" of their own new-felt power.

The attempt by the kingship to establish its own power in the New World and to limit the power of the indigenous landed class and the city-held regional parliamentary councils by setting up surrogate kingships in centralized districts throughout the realm was partially successful for only a short period of time.

Slowly, over the years, the surrogate kingships, or viceroys, passed from being true governorships of the territories over which they were assigned to prestigious but impotent representatives of a distant, weakening power. However, the conquest of Spain by Napoleon and the complete unseating of the Spanish kingship was necessary before actual rebellion against the surrogate kings' authority was undertaken. Even then this rebellion was undertaken hesitantly. For though they ceased to *rule*, their prestige as a mirror of the kingship, symbol of reified authority, and unifier of the realm, and representative of the luxury of courtly aristocratic life, was still held in awe and great esteem by those in the New World.

Nonetheless, long before Napoleon or independence, the viceroys had already yielded political control to those

* An institution and an institutional structure imported from Spain.

who controlled the landed estates and to those who really
knew and manipulated the political, economic, religious,
and social life of the territories both in the countryside
and in the cities.

(4) RELIGIOUS: The church in the New World had again
become a large landholder, as usual. All the purging and
purifying and political subjugation that had occurred in
early inquisitional Spain was *reversed* totally in the New
World. The priesthood became a vested *landed interest*
once again. Priestly estate holdings were vast. The priesthood became worldly and "venal" again, and *linked directly through family ties to the lordly landed class of the
New World* as they had been to that class in the Old
World in pre-inquisitional days.

The Spanish high prelates, appointed by the Spanish
kingship as the religious equivalent to the civil viceroyalties, became exalted but honorific offices, just as the viceroys did, the real power passing to the indigenous churchmen or those Spanish prelates who "bought into," and
identified with, the world of the indigenous landed estate
owners . . .

Thus, instead of acting as the bureaucratic arm of the
kingship as in postinquisitional Spain, the priestly class
aligned and amalgamated with the Latin American semi-
feudal lordly class, and acted as a bastion of that class and
its interests from that point onward. . . .

(5) BUREAUCRATIC: The officials sent by the crown, including in some cases the viceroy himself, tended to stray
from kingly directives and favor the colonists' positions in

their affairs. They could gain land, wealth, and power, and even acquire their own landed estates. They engaged in mining ventures, land speculation and manipulation, bribery, fraud, nepotism—all the bureaucratic devices for gaining wealth and power.

Thus again, rather than serving as the civic bastion of kingly authority, the bureaucratic class in the New World acted in collusion with indigenous interests, and served to undermine rather than establish kingly authority on the new continent.

The attempted abolition of the *encomiendas* could then do nothing but fail in its intent. It could not prevent the establishment of a permanent, powerful, landed class. And, in fact, from this point onward the reform alerted that class to the precariousness of its position. After the reform attempts, the landed class used all its influence and power to attempt to establish permanently its rights of possession, control, and dispensation over its estates.

THE ESTABLISHMENT OF PERMANENTLY HERITABLE ESTATES

In 1555, "to avoid any possible lapse in their grants, a strong effort was made by the colonists to obtain a decree from the King making *encomiendas* perpetual."[6] The kingship and its priestly chief minister, Las Casas, blocked this move temporarily, but to no avail. "For, in 1559, a 'third life' was added . . . in 1607 . . . a 'fourth life' was granted . . . in 1629 . . . a 'fifth life' was added."[7]

Thus, generation after generation during a whole century, the titles to *encomiendas* were extended, with the natural result that they came to be regarded as possessions of the family to which they had originally been assigned.

THE ENTAILED ESTATES ("MAYORAZGOS")

"An institution that played an important role in maintaining these large properties unbroken for several centuries was the system of *mayorazgos*." This was the culmination of the colonists' success against the kingship. After the "New Laws of the Indies," which sought to break up the estates and disinherit the *encomienda* owners, proved a fiasco and impossible to enforce, the kingship gave in to the will of the colonists to form permanent, heritable family estates, and decreed the right of certain *encomienda* estate owners to permanently occupy and hold for their families the land and serfs they had originally been given.

The bestowal of a *permanent* estate upon a given estateholder was called the "entailment" of that estate. Under this term, the estate could neither be removed from its original owner and his family, nor could it ever be divided up in any way. "With a desire to attain high social distinction and preserve an elevated rank in society for their descendants, some of the leading families sought and obtained the entailment of their estates."[8]

"Although the number of these entailed, permanently heritable and undividable estates (*mayorazgos*) was not great, *they represented a power and influence far beyond their numerical strength.* This was because they not only held intact a number of great estates, *but they also set a pattern that was followed by the majority of other estate holders*"[9] not to mention those who aspired to hold estates. "It became the custom to hold properties from one generation to another and to pass them undivided to the eldest son in much the same manner,"[10] as under the system of primogeniture in England and parts of Europe.

"During the colonial period, when a large estate had been formed either by the transformation of an *encomienda* into a manorial 'farm' or by other means, it ordinarily remained unbroken. This stability was due to two facts: first, an *encomienda* could not be divided, and, second, the general practice that developed was to create an 'entailed,' or heritable, undividable, estate whenever possible."[11]

From this point on *the permanent, heritable, indivisible, serf-controlling estate became the symbol of prestige and the claim to aristocracy and nobility for oneself and for one's family.* It became the equivalent of a kingly bestowed title of which none was bestowed on the new continent that was not accompanied by an estate.

"No sooner would a colonist acquire a fortune, whether from trade, mining, the tribute of Indian villages, or the product of his farms, then he would seek a title of nobility and with this title would go the estate, which from then on must remain undivided."[12]

Europe in the postfeudal period and Spain in the reconquest period exhibited a similar direction for ambition and prestige. The knightly style of life with its private empires and serf-lord relationship was the social cynosure of all feudal and semi-feudal societies.

Rewards of land were even more easily obtainable on the new continent than in reconquest Iberia or post-feudal Europe. There was simply more land and more land open to give. Thus, titles usually brought estates with them in contrast, for example, to Iberia and Europe where many lesser nobles who received newly awarded titles, *never* received any land and continued poor, landless, and even town-bound, though technically members of the nobility.

"It was this custom of forming entailed estates that was largely responsible for the preservation of large estates in Latin America. Aggregation was going on constantly; division of property was almost impossible."[13]

What we had in our country was great landowning and autonomous families, lords of the plantation, with an altar and a chaplain in the house and Indians armed with bow and arrow or Negroes armed with muskets at their command. . . .[14]

17

THE PRIESTLY CLASS REPEATS ITS WORLDLY INDULGENT STYLE OF LIFE ON THE NEW CONTINENT

In postinquisitional Spain, after the priesthood had been purged of its worldly, aristocratic character and purged of its semi-feudal knightly origins, it became a segment of the bureaucratic state.

In the conquest of the new continent, the priesthood was there along with the Spanish army to claim the land and its inhabitants for the Spanish kingship. The first frontier settlements were religious missions. The first act of the Spanish conquerors was to Christianize the pagan populations:

Catholic missionaries—Dominicans, Franciscans, or Friars of other orders accompanied every expedition; when a city was founded . . . a priest was always present to bless it; and invariably a church was one of the first buildings to be erected.[1]

The priests provided a cloak of legitimacy for the conquest, and the conquerors thus welcomed them during the early years of bloodshed, rape, and slavery. The Jesuits came early and their missionary zeal, which both converted and pacified the Indians, was welcomed by *conquistador* and establishment prelate alike.

As the early turmoil gave way to a more orderly form of administration, and as the kingship established an orderly colonial government through its viceroys, the priests came to play the same role here that they had played in the Spanish state. They came to form a crucial part of the surrogate kingship's bureaucratic structure for administration of the newly acquired colonies: "The Church, her hierarchy subject to royal patronage, was an instrument of royal control. All agencies of government merely echoed the voice of the king."[2]

At this point, however, the parallel with postinquisitional Spain ends, and a parallel with pre-inquisitional reconquest Spain begins.

We have mentioned that the Spanish kingship successfully purged the Spanish priesthood of its aristocratic ties. Priests were then drawn from ambitious, usually city, merchant middle-class origins, and these priests, owing their entire success to the power and largess of the kingship, threw in their lot with the kingship to become the most loyal of the kingly bureaucrats.

In the New World, on the other hand, a new direction lay open to these men. With land and serfs available, the aristocratic life-style was fully achievable once again in the New World—just at the point where it had been broken in Spain and no longer open to the priesthood or anyone else.

Nobility beckoned, slaves bowed down, eager women awaited conversion, land was waiting to be tilled and pastured, palaces were arising, gold and silver was pouring from the mines . . . the pleasures of the worldly world beckoned . . .

The priests of the New World began to accumulate land and serfs just like the *conquistadores*. The church came to control vast estates rivaling those of the *encomenderos*. In many cases its estates, too, originated from *encomienda* grants. Hundreds of serfs came under priestly control. The building of churches paralleled the building of the "great houses" on the lay estates. Gold and silver were directed into church ornamentation first and then into church coffers. The entire style of the estate lords was gradually adopted by the priestly class. Priestly estates were enlivened with luxuries. Churches grew larger and were more heavily and richly decorated. Coteries of serf-servants jumped at the beck and call of the newly established ecclesiastical lords. Priestly concubinage became common and open. As in reconquest Spain, legitimacy was granted to the priests' heirs who, however, in this case were mestizos.

The priesthood became active in politics and began to act not as bureaucratic representatives of the Spanish kingship but as a vested landed interest fighting for the protection of their lands, their fortunes, their serfs, and their privileges. The priests became allies of the lay lords and enemies of any and all encroachments upon their vested position.

When news of the possibilities of upward mobility for priests in the New World reached Spain, a vast exodus of priests and monks responded and descended upon the new continent. At first the kingship looked upon this response favorably because the postinquisitional priesthood was its closest ally. It was especially Isabella who, during the early years of the colonization, thought that the conversion of the Indians was of prime importance.

By the time the Spanish kingship realized that the priests were not to be relied upon, it was too late for thousands of priests had already emigrated. They were on the way to making their fortunes and there was no way to bring them back. In response the kingship attempted to establish a superordinate structure of high prelates, who would be completely loyal to the Spanish crown, above the vast hordes of priests and monks in America just as they had created a civil superordinate authority over the estate lords with the viceroyalties.

This superordinate Spanish high priesthood acted as part of the viceroyal governorships and exerted some degree of control over priestly economic, political, and social affairs in America. The process of worldly involvement and the aristocratic style of life, however, had already been so powerfully ingrained that no control from Spain was able appreciably to alter the independent action pattern. The Spanish church had come full circle in the New World. It had become worldly and venal during the early years of the reconquest of Spain from the Moslems, had been purged and purified of its worldly and venal ways, and now on the new continent, had once again become worldly, wealthy, and venal. The wheel had come full turn but one vestige of the purified postinquisitional church remained on the new continent; the incorruptible Jesuits with their ascetic, sanctified manners and their utopian projects to protect their unfortunate enslaved Indian wards. Eventually, however, even they would disappear, and their land and their wards would be greedily pounced upon by those secular and religious forces who had forced their withdrawal by the year 1775.*

THE FUSION OF THE LORDLY AND PRIESTLY LANDED CLASSES
The Creation of Entailed Ecclesiastical Estates

In Latin America, "the clergy was an economically privileged class from the beginning. The members of it received large grants of land from the crown. Many monasteries, cathedrals, and individual prelates were given *encomiendas* which have more or less the same history as those conferred upon laymen."[3]

Spain had long been accustomed to this concentration of property in the hands of the church, and, though the kingship, through its Inquisition, and the city merchants, through their parliament, attempted to block such concentrations, "it is said that nearly half of the land in Spain in the 16th century was held by the clergy."[4]

---

* The Jesuits fell when even their estates were coveted by the land-hungry commercial and estate classes. The lucrative commercial-communal estates with their yerba-mate and other export crops were greedily coveted and eventually taken and converted into lord-serf estates. The experiment in paternal-communal, Indian-worked communities yielded, as did all other communities in Latin America, to the latifundia.[5]

Along with this accumulation of propertied estates, ecclesiastical capital was also free from taxation like that of the estate lords in Latin America.*

It is not surprising, then, that "as the years went on, the early missionary fervor tended to give place to complacent well-being,"⁶ as it did in the time of reconquest Spain when similar opportunities presented themselves . . .

It should also be of no surprise that "adventurers were to be found in the ranks of the clergy"⁷ if one remembers that after the Inquisition the clergy had become a line of upward mobility for the ambitious young men of the middle city strata. In addition, it should be remembered that even in the time of the aristocratic church, the priesthood was considered an avenue of political and social opportunity by those aristocrats not fortunate enough to directly inherit their families' estates.

Thus it was that in the New World, "this means of acquiring an honorable position and livelihood attracted such large numbers that in 1644 the parliament convened at Mexico City implored Philip IV to send no more monks, as more than six thousand were without employment, living on the fat of the land." . . .⁸

THE PRIESTHOOD AS LEGITIMATOR OF THE NEW SEMI-FEUDAL ORDER

The priests and the monks were tolerated even though they were seen as a threat and a nuisance. The pacification of the Indians and their permanent subjugation

* In Spain the lords were taxed to some extent.

required a powerful legitimating agency in this world and the promise of a better life in some later world. The reality of the serf, and for that matter of any negatively privileged class, has always been filled with religious rationales explaining away the lifelong misery and injustice they endured. This has always been accompanied by a denial of the body in this world and an exalting of the soul in the next.

Just as the Brahmins were absolutely necessary to the Indian kings for maintaining their superordinate caste status, so, too, was the Christian priesthood necessary for maintaining the superordinate status of the Spanish lordly class. And just as the Brahminate became merged with the Indian upper strata, so, too, the Christian priesthood became merged with the Latin American upper strata.*

As long as many of the chiefs and kings of the Indian empires still lived, the possibility of massive rebellion by the enserfed Indians still faced the early Spanish settlers.† Therefore the carriers of legitimation and pacification were welcomed by all the Spanish settlers in the early years of the colonization. A priest was placed on every manor, a church in every town, and missionaries were sent out to all the unincorporated villages. "Indians were baptized by the thousand, apparently accepting without much inconvenience the new priests who replaced their own."⁹

---

* This was true also of the role of Zen in Japan and Southeast Asia. I have no space for further examples here, but this old, and now vulgarized, doctrine has much validity.

† The rebellion of the last living Inca emperor, and other such uprisings, were still fresh in their memories.

Interestingly, a fusion of Christian and pagan religious symbols occurred in Latin America, providing a continuity with the past as well as a legitimization and solidification of the then present situation. This occurred in a fashion similar to the original evolutionary process of the Christian religion, in which the fusion of the Jewish symbols first with new Roman pagan, then with North European pagan, symbolisms formed the body of the newly emergent religion and provided a similar kind of link with the past and legitimation of the present.*

Thus Christianity, originally formed amidst the destruction of the Roman empire and later becoming the chief legitimator of the European feudal structure, was introduced into Latin America during the destruction of the American Indian empires and became the chief legitimator of the Latin American semi-feudal order.

In this context, during the first few centuries of the Spanish colonization of Latin America, the excesses of the priesthood were overlooked and their holy mission of conversion of the newly conquered Indian populations was both encouraged and venerated.

THE FUSION OF PRIESTLY AND LORDLY INTERESTS

The church's sources of revenue were numerous and diverse. In addition to the customary sums received from

* The Pauline doctrines of original sin and the resurrection, of course, sent Christianity on a separate course from Judaism, but here I am referring to its further evolution in its adoption by the Romans and the post-Roman, pre-feudal Europeans.

tithes and the performance of the sacraments the church used the *personal services and labor of the Indians without limit.* * It will be remembered that after the expulsion of the Jews from Spain, the Christian priestly class became the main body of *scholar-legists* in the realm, so that large sums were also gained from the clergy's legal practice in both civil and ecclesiastical courts. *"The clergy also operated and controlled grocery stores and meat markets and engaged in commerce of all sorts."*[10]

In addition, direct usurpation, especially of Indian lands, by the clergy was by no means unusual. This accumulation of real property by the clergy began in the colonial era, and as generation succeeded generation, the church came to control more and more of the land of the emerging Latin American counntries. "The total property of the secular and regular clergy [of Mexico] was not less than half of the total value of the real estate in the country."[11]

In fact, the priestly class became in every way similar to the class of secular estate lords. Their interests became the same and their actions became similar. Before long it was not the Spanish priesthood that dominated the Latin American church, but the sons of the estate lords, who, sharing the style of life and aspirations of the priesthood and moving in the same sociopolitical circles, came to be the natural heirs to the priestly domains.

Thus even before independence, the control of ecclesiastical estates and wealth, along with the control of secu-

---

* Even the Jesuits did this, though in a humane manner, but with the same result, the enhancement and enrichment of their order.

lar estates and wealth, fell to the same class. The secular and religious *encomendero* estate-holders became one from a fusing of interests between secular and religious landed interests. The aristocrats of the secular and religious landed estates were drawn from the same circle of families. There was now one landed aristocratic interest, related by blood, and the division between the secular and the religious which had been crucial in the politics of feudal and postfeudal Europe* was, in Latin America, a purely semantic separation.†

---

  * In Spain the division between church and state—so much a part of European political activities—was ended by the Inquisitional subordination of the clergy to the kingship. However, the independence of the Spanish church was reasserted in the late eighteenth century after the crumbling of the Spanish kingship, and again became a crucial political factor there.[12]

  † Until conditions of the mid-twentieth century again altered the external and internal relationships of the church, this situation remained. It is not surprising to find, then, that those who would later be opposed to the estate lords, would also be anticlerical as well.

18

THE CREATION OF SEMI-FEUDAL ESTATES FROM SOURCES OTHER THAN "ENCOMIENDA" GRANTS: THE EXTENSION OF SMALL HOLDINGS

Some of the landed estates owe their origin to other forms of grant. Not all Spaniards who came to Latin America after the conquest were accommodated with large tribute districts. "There were many who, for one reason or another, received outright grants of land, but without serfs."[1]

These grants were of two kinds: *peonías* and *caballerías*, so called originally because they were rewards to soldiers of the two arms of the service, the *peonía* (infantry) and the *caballería* (mounted troops). The same terms had been used earlier to designate the rewards that were given to soldiers who aided in the reconquest of Spain from the Moslems.

"The *peonía* . . . was supposed to represent the total amount of land, orchard, agricultural, and grazing lands, sufficient to maintain a single family in modest circumstances. It would probably comprise something over 100

187

acres, varying, however, according to the character of the land."[2]

Persons of greater merit were to be given an allotment of land five times that of the *peonía*. "The *caballería* comprised, apparently, some 165 acres of arable land, with pasture sufficient to support over 700 cattle of different kinds. The entire grant would probably contain from 500–1,000 acres of land, according to its character. This was called the *caballería*, although it was apparently not restricted, in the colonies, to mounted troops,"[3] but given freely as reward to anyone gaining the favor of the viceroy or king for prowess in battle or loyal services rendered. Often it was gained through squatters' economic development, which the Spanish kingship found it necessary to recognize. In practice, "improvement, and four years of occupancy were enough to give full title to the property."[4]

It is evident that the *caballería* was a land acquisition made open to all politically, militarily, or economically ambitious individuals on the new continent. It may also be seen that the fluid ease with which such land might be granted and claimed allowed for the establishment of a precedent, so that once such a grant was made, the recipient of that grant could use it as the first step toward expansion through the extension of economic activity beneficial to the kingship, or through political manipulation, or through outright military takeover of surrounding lands and peoples. This is precisely the pattern that did develop out of the loose, fluid, ill-defined system of *cabal-*

lería grants in the New World. Such a situation existed also in reconquest Spain, but was eventually closed off by the kingship in its attempt to destroy the growing power of the semi-feudal estate lords. One should also remember that neither good land for occupancy nor readily conquerable peoples existed in Iberia in anywhere near the colossal proportions in which they existed in Latin America.

"In the long run these grants formed the nucleus about which the recipients accumulated additional holdings. The means by which this aggrandizement was effected were various, but consisted usually in the seizure of Indian holdings, in marrying Indian women who were owners of property, or in the occupation of unclaimed lands."[5]

The Spaniard's desire to be a lord demanded this kind of land expansion, rather than economically *intensive* concentration on the commercial production of food. For it was not commercial profit that was sought by these Spanish colonists, but freedom from manual labor and the knightly style of life in its entirety. Land expansion meant estate creation, and estate creation meant the incorporation of Indian villages for serf-labor. Spaniards preferred to seek a subsistence agricultural and artisan manorial estate, to a commercially productive, market-linked "farm." The goal of this estate creation was sociopolitical rather than economic.

A useful comparison may be made between the cattle barons of the arid plains in the southwest of North America and the estate-builders of Latin America. Given the land conditions of much of Latin America, economically intensive agriculture was impossible anyway, and land extension was the only possible expansionist process available. Where this was the case in North America, a similar process and social structure occurred.

This last comparison should be qualified by the fact that where the possibility of intensive agriculture *did* exist, it was not taken by the Spanish colonists, but subsistence estate creation was undertaken in any case. In fact, intensive agriculture was not undertaken until German, Italian, Slavic, Japanese, and Chinese farmers in turn attempted this quite successfully in the early twentieth century.

Thus a comparison of the Latin American Spaniards' knightly aversion to work and economic profit with the North American Puritan dependence upon work and profit as salvation and a sign of grace, though stereotyped and sterile as used in the typical historical comparison, was, and still is to a large extent, factually correct, if placed in its proper structural context and if moral connotations are averted.

THE CREATION OF SEMI-FEUDAL ESTATES FROM STILL OTHER SOURCES

Some estates are said to have been created from the holdings of the Indian chieftains (*cacicazgos*) and nobles. These lands, if held with tenanted (tribute-bound) serfs attached, as seems to have been the case in certain instances, would easily have been converted into *senorías* (semi-feudal fiefs), with which the Spaniards had been familiar in their own country.

Upon such holdings the colonists merely replaced the fallen Indian nobility as overlords. "Zorita, writing about 1560, says that 'all the Indian nobility have now lost their lands, their serfs (*mayeques*), and their renters, and are very poor.' These lands the Spaniards treated as legitimate spoils of war, and they were appropriated to form the estates of the conquerors."[6]

THE NEW WORLD ORIGINS OF THE LEGITIMACY OF THE MESTIZO*

Marriage as a Form of Land Acquisition

Aside from direct military conquest, "one way in which land acquisition and transfer of ownership came about was through the intermarriage between estate owners and the natives. Some of the Spaniards did not disdain formal marriage with the Indians, particularly with the daughters of nobles and village and tribal headmen, or any other marriage that would result in land."[7]

"These relationships brought the Spaniards at once into the status of membership in the kinship groups with the concomitant rights to the community possessions."[8] This relationship worked to the advantage of both the Indian kinship group and the Spaniard involved for the Spaniard

---

* See Ch. 2 for "old world" origins of the legitimacy of the mestizo.

inherited the Indian clan-lands, his original motivation for
the marriage, and the Indian clan was able to maintain
some political and social status through the daughter married to the Spaniard, and especially, through the children
of the union who were often recognized as the legitimate
heirs to the estate lands.

The Indian clans, however, usually maintained their
advantage for just one generation, for the mestizo children, in an attempt to gain total legitimacy as part of the
conquering strata, invariably disidentified with the Indian
side of their family and reduced them to serfdom to insure
their own lordly status.

On the other hand, it was true that the Spaniard who
married into the clan gained not only clan-heritable lands,
but also a kind of legitimacy without which the complete
maintenance of the emerging semi-feudal social structure
might not have been possible in a land of two ethnic and
racially distinct peoples. That is, "with the mingling of
the two races that took place as settlement became more
general, it was not long before the owners of the estates
had among the Indians who were attached to them many
in whose veins their own blood was diffused. They thus
came to occupy the position more like that of a patriarch,"[9] or clan head, similar to the positions often held by
princes from conquering tribes previous to the Spanish
arrival.

Thus a certain legitimacy gleaned from within the
kinship units of the conquered peoples was gained by the
conquering Spanish lord, and a biological as well as social

tie was formed, so that the Spanish conqueror also became father of the clans (later "father" of the estate
serfs). His sons and daughters (the mestizos), gleaning
some of his legitimacy, gave their allegiance to the conquering lord wholeheartedly in the hopes of gaining a
positively privileged status in contrast to that of the serfs.
This was an attempt and desire to gain actual political
and social power as the heirs apparent to the lord's, their
father's, estate and title.

This entire process was facilitated by the fact that such
mingling and legitimacy patterns were already pre-estab-
lished in reconquest Spain where Moslem, Jewish, and
Christian intermarriage was common among the upper
classes and where even illegitimacy was *not* frowned upon,
given the nature of the pre-inquisition churchmen's pen-
chant for retaining mistresses and bestowing legitimacy
upon offsprings of such unions.

Added to the above, as Gilberto Freyre has stated so
poetically, the Indian women resembled in build and
color the Moslem women who were held in highest
esteem among the Iberians; thus the acceptance of them
and their offspring was facilitated by the past social-cul-
tural context, rather than inhibited by it as was the case in
Puritan white-superiority-oriented North America.* In

* "Long contact with the Saracens had left with the Portuguese the
idealized figure of the 'enchanted Moorish woman,' a charming type,
brown-skinned, black-eyed, enveloped in sexual mysticism, roseate in hue,
and always engaged in combing out her hair or bathing in rivers or in the
waters of haunted fountains; and the Brazilian colonizers were to
encounter practically a counterpart of this type in the naked Indian

almost all respects the preconditions of the mingling of the two races, and the legitimacy pattern that occurred, was facilitated rather than inhibited.

This kind of legitimacy rarely occurred in North America. First, because the Puritan background prohibited it; second, because among scattered hunting tribes with no permanent settlements or high population densities to hold or claim lands, it was unnecessary to form such involvements. It was easier just to scatter or remove the hunting peoples. And third, in the American south where estates *were* formed, the Africans had neither clan nor lands to produce the necessity for such legitimated unions, and the Protestant background of the "lords" strictly forbade even the possibility of legitimating such unions. When they did occur the form was hidden, guilt-ridden concubinage with completely unrecognized kinship ties. Children of these unions neither gained legitimacy nor became heirs to anything but moral indignation and shame.

When African slaves were brought to the tropical estates of Latin America, they were integrated into an already functioning legitimacy and social structure, so that, though they possessed no lands, they were incorporated similarly to the Indians in that sexual unions often

---

women with their loose-flowing hair. These latter also had dark tresses and dark eyes and bodies painted red, and, like the Moorish nereids, were extravagantly fond of a river bath to refresh their ardent nudity, and were fond, too, of combing their hair. . . . Only, they were a little less coy. . . ." (Freyre: *Masters and Slaves*, p. 19.)

produced marriages. The slaves were rapidly converted to serf status and looked upon the lord as their biological patriarch as well as estate lord; and mulattos often gained legitimacy as the heirs to the estates as well as the social and political power that came with that social legitimacy. It was for this reason that mulatto and mestizo came to occupy similar positions in the social structure, often mingling sexually and maritally. For the same reason the Africans came to occupy the same position as the Indians, that is, negatively privileged serfs, cut off from legitimacy and mobility in the social structure, and socially isolated from the other classes and from each other.

LAND ALIENATION IN LATIN AMERICA

Estate Formation Through the "Purchase" of Indian Lands

After the conquest in the more remote territories and in the more remote districts of the settled territories, there was still quite a bit of land retained by the Indians, yet relatively little used by them. Most of this "unused" land was grazing land, for though the Indians did domesticate llamas and alpacas, herding for large-scale meat consumption was by no means well developed by them.

Thus a situation presented itself after the *encomiendas* and land grants were all given out, where many Spaniards found themselves landless, and where available (though not the best) lands existed which were held by the Indians, but only loosely and sporadically used.

One should add to this situation that the Spaniards were experienced herdsmen, especially at sheep-grazing. One should also remember that sheep-grazing was considered so crucial to the Spanish economy, that no enclosure laws were ever passed in Spain.* Add to this that the land itself and the climatic conditions were often similar to those of the dry plateaus of Spain. The Spaniards were thus skilled at grazing, and pasture lands were available, the lands having a remarkable similarity to those of Spain in terms of climatic and soil conditions. The land-hungry, estate-hungry, status-hungry Spaniards, as well as mestizos, cast envious glances at the "unused" lands.

The Indians, like all pre-industrial peoples, lived under a reality and social structure in which all lands were held by the clans of the villages or the hunting bands that utilized and inhabited any given territory. Now, the clans and clan-clusters always held more land than they were using at any given time, since hunting and agricultural techniques were as yet limited in terms of intensive production on any given defined land area, except on the shores of the flooding lakes where the first American civilizations grew. But those lands were already taken by the Spaniards, or, as in the case of the Andean highlands,

---

* As opposed to England where the enclosures played so crucial a role in the elimination of the peasantry, the growth of the commercial gentry in the countryside, and the destruction of the entire feudal order itself.

those who held the knowledge with which to harness the waters and intensively utilize the lands were murdered by the Spaniards in the early part of the conquest. Almost the entire Inca aristocracy was put to death either in battle, after capture, or later by piratical gold seekers, and their knowledge and technical skills for intensive land and animal cultivation and production, as well as their miraculous distributional and economic organizational skills, were lost to the Indian serfs who remained. Since the serfs never held this knowledge, nor the knowledge of warfare, or religion, this knowledge being class-bound as in all urban-centered, rigidly stratified, prebureaucratic* empires, it was lost when the upper strata were destroyed.

This knowledge was not only lost to the Indian serfs who remained after their upper strata had been decimated (since it was kept from them always by the priestly and

* The Indian empire was just approaching the bureaucratic stage; as yet, as in all early civilizations, knowledge resided only in the priestly and military upper strata, commoners were not yet brought in as bureaucrats, for such a stage of size and complexity had not yet been reached. Captive slaves and indigenous serfs still formed the backbone of the economy. Thus, unlike China and Arabia, where knowledge was held and developed by the bureaucratic class and thus preserved when the ruling classes were removed, in the Indian empires, knowledge still resided in the upper strata, and their removal totally destroyed those civilizations as civilizations. The technical knowledge of Egypt still resides with the priestly and military classes interred in the tombs of the kings, for there, too, a bureaucratic class—though growing—never developed to the point of usurping this technical knowledge as did those bureaucratic classes of the Middle East and Far East later. (See also the modern trend toward usurpation of technical knowledge and skills by the German bureaucrats in the nineteenth century. See also the present-day trend of the bureaucratic class for the absorption and propagation of all technical skills.)

military clans in order to keep them as serfs), but it was lost to the Spaniards as well, who initiated sheep and cattle-grazing and cash-crop production later on, but who never have been able or willing to re-create the intensive surplus-subsistence agricultural system employed by the empire Indians.

After a century of military conquest and the complete disorganization and dissipation of the knowledge and skills of the Indian civilizations, communal land tenure and more primitive productive techniques formed the basis of the reality and social system of the remaining Indians.

The Indians, then, had returned in large measure to a more primitive agricultural system of landholding and food production. As we have said, this pre-empire system demanded a situation where far more territory had to be held in the clans' name than it ever could utilize at any given time.

This land, though never all occupied at any given time, was somewhat clearly demarcated by the village-holders, and even by the hunting bands in terms of hunting grounds.* It was to the unused portions of communally held lands that the Spaniards without land turned.

The non-lordly Spaniards used several techniques to obtain these lands from the Indians. Actually they defrauded the Indians since the latter never understood, until it was too late, that the lands were not still theirs.

Firstly, they purchased the land titles from the crown

* As in North America and in Chile.

or from the colonial administrators, and forced the eviction of the resident Indians who were then resettled as tenants on their own previously held lands, or removed completely and enserfed elsewhere. "Such transfers of land from Indians to Spaniards were supposed to be made only after the approval of the viceroy had been obtained. However, with the disorder that prevailed in the early years of the Spanish domination, the land titles thus acquired were frequently 'imperfect' (falsified, forged, altered), as subsequent events showed."[10]

Secondly, Spaniards engaged in various forms of bribery, trickery, and negotiation in order to actually purchase from naive, corrupt, or sometimes wily Indian village headmen, communal lands that seemed temporarily unused, unnecessary, or useless to the villagers.

Three processes were actually going on in this connection. In the typical, and by far the most common transaction, the Spaniard offered some kind of cash or barter item which the Indians considered valuable (blankets, horses, whiskey, jewelry). In return the Spaniards demanded the ownership of the then unused village lands. This the villagers were willing to give the Spaniard, for in their reality structure it meant that the Spaniard now had the use of this land and would either continue to pay tribute to the village for its continued use or would return it to the village clan cluster. Since no notion of transfer of ownership of clan lands existed in the Indians' reality, since these Spaniards were not taking the land by military force, no reason for suspicion occurred to the villagers and they thought, on the contrary, that they had gotten the better of the deal. They thought that they still held the lands which in their eyes were inalienable except by forceful appropriation—and that they were receiving a tribute-tax for its use, a procedure which they were familiar with from the Indian empires. In the beginning, they did not even balk at their tenant status as part-time laborers for the Spaniards, because this too was part of the social reality and structure of the Indian empires, productive labor being exchanged for military security and economic specialization.

Therefore, thinking they had gotten a fair exchange, the Indians fell prey to the Spaniards, who then had legal title to the Indian lands which the Indians thought they had "rented" out.* The Indians' naïveté had operated against them in this kind of case, and great chunks of communal lands were alienated from their clan-village owners in this way. This was the most characteristic form of land alienation to occur in Latin America; and it became the most typical pattern of commercial land accumulation in all the pre-industrial clan-village areas of the world.†

The second type of land alienation involved the bribery of corrupt village headmen. This was far less common, but did occur. The chiefs of the villages had lost much of their prestige after their humiliating and rapid defeat at

---

* Applicable to the purchase of Manhattan Island from the Indians of North America.

† Such as Asia and Africa.

the hands of the Spaniards. Therefore many sought to refurbish their fallen image, while others sought to retreat from it.

In the first instance the Spaniards brought gifts such as Arabian stallions and Oriental silks for the downcast headmen. The possession of such magnificent steeds or attire did much to revive the spirits of the once venerated clan heads. In return they were more than willing to sign away lands which had become useless to the maintenance of their headman status anyway. Such bribery was not uncommon, and these chieftains were not denounced by their followers who also took pride and rejoiced that their headman once again rode proud and dressed richly. They, too, could hold their heads high if they were graced with such a leader. So these headmen became empty symbols of a once-known glorious past, and their followers venerated rather than derided them.

In the second instance, the headman lived in such shame at his ignominious position, that nothing could raise his spirit except spirits . . . and he retreated into his own private world. The Spaniards' wines and whiskies could whisk him there quicker than anything he had previously known. These were the brooders, the demoralized chieftains who sat alone, staring skyward, dreaming of the glories of the past and their once-held power. The Spaniards exploited such headmen by supplying the "spirit water" for their retreatism, and in return received the land titles they were after.* The villagers in this case

* Typical of North America, of course.

lived in shame for their leaders and for their own status, but usually resigned themselves to their fate, harboring resentment against the Spaniards, while blaming the gods and themselves for their poor fate. The turning of the blame and the harnessing of the resentments was not to occur for three centuries.

Thirdly, wily village headmen often thought they were tricking the Spaniards by bartering off large tracts of land which their clans held, but which they considered useless. Since the importation of sheep and cattle did not reach the more remote Indian villages for quite a time, they often willingly and, they thought, cunningly, gave up rocky pasture land which they did not need. The Spaniards, of course, knew just what they were getting, and took this land gleefully, for they knew the value of good grazing lands.

In this way many mountain-dwelling agricultural villagers lost large tracts of clan-held lands, and the Spaniards moved in to form ranchos and estates in these areas. In fact, as the Spaniards incorporated more and more of this land, and encroached completely on the agricultural settlements, young man after young man was forced out of his village, due to lack of agricultural and land-expansion possibilities, and onto the stock-raising estates as cowboys and shepherds. In this manner, the lands of the unincorporated villages dwindled and their ranks shrank, and ever greater percentages of the Indians became incorporated into the structure of the great semi-feudal estates.

Lastly, lands were also "leased" from Indian villages

with time stipulations on the deeds, but time and serf-seeking colonial officials soon made permanent most of these deeds so that the land was permanently alienated from the communal villages.

Into the disorganized malaise of the years of conquest, the landless Spaniards moved as the empire Indian military aristocrats once had moved. But now, instead of enslaving and enserfing the village Indians in order to produce a tightly organized, centralized political system with an integrated, highly technically developed and coordinated economic structure, the Spaniards enslaved and enserfed the Indians in order to create private, jurisdictionally separated, politically distinct, feudal subsistence, or later, export-oriented, estates.

The process of land conquest and *incorporation* practiced by the Indian nobility became land purchase and *separation* as practiced by the Spaniards aspiring to semi-feudal aristocratic status. To the empire Indian the process was famailir, but unknown to them at the time, the political and economic result was to be quite different. To the non-empire Indians, the process was as bewildering as the results were abhorrent.

The process of land alienation from Indian clan-communal villages was accelerated one hundredfold in the commercial period of the late nineteenth century and early twentieth century, with resultant tremendous social and political ramifications.*

* As it had produced in the same period in Asia and Africa.

19

THE TRIUMPH OF THE LORDS AND PRIESTS OF THE PRIVATE SEMI-FEUDAL ESTATES

"The legislation abolishing the *encomiendas* actually brought but slight change in conditions so far as the lives of those living under this system were concerned. The relationship of Lord and Serf which had grown up during the several centuries in which the *encomiendas* had continued to mold Latin American society was not destroyed. The *encomendero* disappeared, but the *hacendado* had already taken his place."[1]

The Indian too no longer existed. He had fled back to the forests or the highlands or merged by intermarriage with his conqueror. What had been an Indian existed as the serf laborer, bound by contract or custom to the soil of the great rural properties that the invaders had carved out of the lands of his Indian ancestors. Both the lord and the serf were now Americans, neither Indian nor European though they belonged to two sharply divided classes, each with its own cultural heritage.

The hacienda, which was an outgrowth of both the *encomienda* and land grants of the early days, had become both a territorial and a social unit, consisting of land and the laborers attached to that land.* It had become the dominant institution of Latin America. It served as the basic economic unit as well, and around it, more than around any other form of agricultural holding or mine or factory or commercial center, the economic life of the people was organized. The separation of lord and serf gave caste to the entire social structure. It sharply distinguished upper and lower classes. *It was the relationship that prevailed between these two individuals and classes that determined the type of governmental institutions that existed or could exist in the country.* . . .

LORD AND SERF, THE YEAR, 1936[2]

"I met them on the country road, Don Fulano and his servant (*mozo-squire*), the latter riding at a respectful distance behind. Don Fulano was mounted on a tall, beautiful dapple-gray mare. The squire (*mozo*) rode a much smaller horse of the somewhat shaggy mountain type, a real country nag but a good traveler withal.† Both men used Chilean saddles. Don Fulano's was made of handsome leather, and the seat was covered with the soft, down-clad skin of a large mountain bird. His stirrups . . . were ornamented with bands of iron and inlaid silver. His bridle too . . . bore elaborate silver ornaments about the bit and the brow band. . . . The squire's (*mozo's*) accoutrement was simple, a thick sheepskin covering the

---

* In typical semi-feudal fashion.
† A reflection of the Don Quixote image—and its metaphoric value for Latin American political life.

uncomfortable wooden frame of his saddle, while bridle and riding whip were made of rough-tanned leather thongs.

"Don Fulano was well clad in riding habit with puttees and boots carefully polished. . . . The appearance of his riding companion was in sharp contrast. Not in rags by any means, but cheaply clad underneath his coarsely woven poncho, with ill-fitting trousers, an ungainly short jacket, a dilapidated felt hat and well worn shoes, the *mozo* (squire-servant) could be seen at once as belonging to a different class.

"The servant (*mozo*) waited in silence and at a little distance while Don Fulano greeted us . . . in the same deferential manner and with many repetitions of '*Si, Si, Señor,*' he corroborated his master's detailed orders for our reception on the estate. . . . Glancing back I saw the squire (*mozo*) fall into position behind his master as the two rode leisurely along between the lines of Lombardy poplars that almost met over the country road. . . ."

THE SERF

"He was ten years older than his lord patron and during the latter's childhood had frequently acted in the capacity of guardian and companion of the little fellow who had now grown into proprietorship of the family estate."*

---

* The servant raising the lord was typical of semi-feudal arrangements. This was the custom during the Russian Tzarist period after the collapse of the Turkish empire.

"The serf's father and grandfather had been born on this estate. His mother's family, too, had lived on a distant part of the same property for as many generations as they could recall. As a consequence they all felt an interest in the work to be done out of all proportion to the meager compensation they derived from it. (Like most serfs—their serf right and other traditional attachment to their manorial estate was great.)

"The lord and the serf were both born on the estate. The latter had never lived elsewhere; in fact he had seldom been away from his home place for more than a day or two at a time. He had begun his duties as son of a tenanted serf when about seven years old. When he had reached the age of ten he was spending most of his time in care of the sheep belonging to the estate . . .

"When he was a boy, there had been no school upon the estate and the nearest village was miles away. So he grew to manhood with no opportunity . . . to learn to read and write. He was thus illiterate, though far from ignorant, a man thoroughly versed in the lore of his limited habitat, but knowing little beyond the bounds of the estate on which he lived.

"His experience in civic affairs consisted of but few incidents. Once he had been sent into town with most of the other serfs of the estate to vote on a measure that affected the property. He had for this occasion painstakingly learned to write his name and had put his signature where told on a sheet of paper. . . . Such had been the life of his father, his grandfather, and of as many generations as could be remembered. None of them had known any other condition than that of a hereditary tenantry."

THE LORD

"The Señora, Don Fulano's gracious wife, presided; and his family of eight children . . . gathered quietly at their places. A French governess completed the group. Several maids assisted the Señora or looked after the smaller children. The conversation about the table was carried on in three languages* . . . Refined courtesy prevailed throughout the meal, except when one or two of the younger children found it necessary to raise their voices in command when a servant demurred at complying with all their wishes.

"Don Fulano began his career by learning to command. Almost before he could walk or talk he had learned that he could impose his will on most of the circle around him. Servants attended him from dawn until night. His parents he learned to respect and love, and among his large family of brothers and sisters he found that he had met his peers."† "Outside of this group his wish was usually law."

"He had no set tasks that he must do; every labor was done for him; he moved a small King in his small world. . . .

---

* Spanish, English, and German (for the administrator of the estate). (Foreign Administrators will be discussed.)

† The importance of family relations—inter and intra—is a factor in Latin American politics.

"The situation changed somewhat when at an early age he was put into a private school in the city. A servant accompanied him to the school in the morning and was waiting for him at the end of the day, even carrying his books the few blocks between school and home. . . . Until he was nearly twenty years of age, most of his time had been spent in school, first under a governess in their city home, then in the priests' school, later in the capital of his country, where also a family residence was maintained, and at last in two years of study in France. Most of his education had been in letters and arts. He had never studied agriculture or administration.

"During the period of schooling, vacations had been spent on the estate where, in association with his father, he had become familiar with some of the problems of its management. He had never done any manual work. His hands had never turned a shovelful of earth, nor had he followed a plow, nor milked a cow, nor yoked a team of oxen . . . his training and experience had fitted him only to direct, to command."*

. . . "After his education was completed he had begun a desultory practice of law that very soon brought him into political life. Here the influence of family and friends together with the prestige of his wealth had led to rapid advance. He had occupied many official positions, most of them under the national government. He had served as prefect of his province, as deputy in congress, and was

* During the Russian Revolution, the way one distinguished an aristocrat from a commoner was by looking at his hands.

now senator for one of the neighboring provinces in which his family was very influential."

"From this class also were recruited most of those who entered the learned professions. The clergy, the university professors, the literary lights, the artists, the lawyers, the medical men, the politicians and statesmen were mostly drawn from this group. It was a leisure class whose members entered such careers rather as dilettantes than from the necessity of earning a livelihood."*

". . . His wife was the daughter of a distant relative (typical of aristocracy). Through her he had come into possession of a second estate not many miles from his home. He tried to be at one of these estates, or both, at planting time and harvest; but even this was not always possible, and the estates were left largely in the hands of the administrators."

"*Don Fulano was, in fact, a city dweller* most of the year, rather than a country resident, a gentleman land owner rather than a farmer. This had been the character of his father before him and of each generation *back nearly four hundred years* to the *conquistador* from whom they proudly traced their descent and from whose grant of land from the Spanish crown their estates had been formed."

* In entering political life, the clergy, or the army, the English landed gentry was doing the same thing—amateurism being their ethic rather than degrading professionalism. Even Weber affirmed amateurism in politics (in *Class, Status, and Party*). The Junker gentry accordingly were seen by him as making the best—least corrupt—politicians, not having to be dependent on politics for a living.

"Thus, there has existed in Latin America a social structure built on a distinctly agrarian basis, and the nation's entire lives have been molded by relation to the land. The landowner has commanded, a landless people has obeyed. A man's status has been determined by whether or not he owned an estate or, at least, by whether he belonged to a land-holding family. Position in life, occupation, opportunity depended mainly on this. Possession of ability, attainment in education, achievement in any line, *even acquisition of wealth* has meant less than being born into a circle that monopolized the land resources of the nation."

". . . Here exists, then, a New World . . . with the social organization of old Spain; a twentieth century people still preserving a feudal society; republics with a blue-blooded aristocracy and a servile class as distinctly separated as in any of the monarchies of the Old World. Throughout Latin America's history this situation has existed. It is this social heritage that forms the background for the present-day problems of the Latin American people. . . ."[3]

PART III

The Development of Cities and Towns in Latin America

20

THE SPANISH CITIES AND TOWNS RE-CREATED ON THE NEW CONTINENT

The Spanish social structure was a unique blend of Moslem empire features and European feudalism. One of the key features preserved from the Moslem days was the maintenance of the great and splendorous capital cities of the regional Moslem kingly rulers. You may also remember that no such luxury cities existed in Northern Europe where the cities were bare, commercially oriented market towns devoid of luxury entertainment and living quarters, and that the existence of such luxury centers in Spain had unique ramifications for the Spanish social structure, altering it drastically from the true feudal model of Europe.

The great cities the Moslems had left behind were maintained, expanded, and further rendered luxurious by the Spaniards. As the centers of political intrigue and social excitements, the cities drew to themselves all of the lords of the realm previously based in the rural areas. Just such a process occurred in Latin America with similar ramifications as those that had occurred in reconquest Spain.

In Latin America, the Spaniards adopted the same policy toward city building and maintenance that they had in Spain. After the initial plundering of the Indian empire capital cities, these cities were refurbished, revitalized, and luxuriated, and new cities were built in crucial economic and political locations where no old ones had previously existed.

The Indian capital cities became the first seats of the viceroys and their courtly and bureaucratic entourage. Where the Europeans could not live, such as at Cuzco, the Inca capital in the high rarified Andean plateau, new capital cities were built, such as Lima, in a climatic and economic setting more congenial to the European style of life and physiology.*

New cities sprang up everywhere—ports, regional capitals, kingly court centers. Everywhere the Spaniards carried their rural social structure, they carried with them also their unique urban social structure.

"The conquest of Latin America . . . led to a redistribution of the inhabitants and to the formation of new centers of population. No sooner had the country been pacified than the Spaniards inaugurated a policy of founding new cities. Some of these, such as Mexico, Tlaxcala, and Texcoco in Mexico, were, it is true, nothing more than the reorganization of existing cities, but a great many were erected upon new sites."[1]

Although the first settlements on the frontier were usually in the form of priestly missions or military out-

---

* The Indians had a special lung and blood-cell adaptation permitting them to exist in the highland areas.

posts or ports of call, all of these were regarded as temporary organizations which, it was expected, would eventually give place to cities.

THE INSTITUTIONAL FORMS OF THE SPANISH CITIES TRANSFERRED TO LATIN AMERICA

The institutional structure of the Spanish cities was
unique in that it combined certain features of empire
capital cities with features derived from the French
feudal, separated-incorporated, merchant market-cities.
The splendor and political-center qualities of the former
were blended with the politically independent and self-
administrative aspects of the latter. This unique Spanish
composite was to be reproduced in Latin America.

   The cities of Castile (the dominant province of Spain
and the administrative headquarters for Spanish affairs in
the "Indies"*) became the model for all Latin American
cities. "Royal orders issued by Charles V and Philip II
(the successors to Ferdinand and Isabella) provided regulations to be followed in the establishment of cities,
towns, and villages."[2]

THE SPANISH CITIES AS LANDHOLDING BODIES

"The cities of Castile had been, from very ancient times,
landholding bodies, possessing more or less extensive ter-

---

* Castile was Isabella's province; Aragon, Ferdinand's province, was
the headquarters for European affairs. The Portuguese cities and administrative structure were similar to Spain's.

ritories."[3] The Spanish cities could be seen almost as city-states, in the Italian sense. They were, to be exact, transitional forms between the completely indepedent Italian city-states and the relatively autonomous incorporated market-cities of North Europe.

"Every city and town had what were known as *propios,* lands owned by the city or town itself and administered by the city officials."[4] This institutional structure was transferred by careful design to the New World, and these city common lands became crucial in Latin America. The offices governing them became important as well, for not all the Spaniards were able to get estates or serfs in the New World, and those who could not remained city-bound and were forced to exploit the civic, political, and economic possibilities of the cities in order to establish power and prestige in the newly conquered continent.

Throughout the colonial period in Latin America, expansion into hitherto unoccupied parts of Latin America was generally accompanied by the founding of landholding cities, enclaves, almost city-states, separated in their jurisdictional boundaries from the private semi-feudal estates, as in Spain.* "These landholding cities established by the Spaniards formed one of the recognized features of the social structure . . ."[5]

---

* This characteristic feature had been borrowed from the historically peculiar separation of merchant market-cities from knightly held fief lands which had occurred in late feudal Europe and had been adopted by the Spaniards under the influence of the French during the years of occupation of the non-Moslem north of Spain.

THE DEVELOPMENT OF REGIONAL PARLIAMENTS AT REGIONAL CAPITAL CITIES: THE CORTES AND THE "CABILDO"

In Spain, as in Italy, France, England, and most of Northern Europe, a peculiar political institution—*the estate council*—emerged in the postfeudal period.

The postfeudal period is often called the *estate-state* period.* This designation refers to the fact that in this period a unique balance of powers between contending classes had occurred where neither the receding feudal classes (knights and peasants) nor the ascending commercial classes (merchants, merchant-gentry, artisans, and free farmers) could neutralize or control the other. At this same time, and deeply involved in this power balance, the rapidly centralizing, kingly bureaucratic state structure was emerging and involving itself in various power alliances with the contending classes.

Facilitated by the mood of compromise engendered by the rapid, expansive economic growth of the period, the estate council arose out of an amalgam of the elective affinities of the contending classes and out of the necessities demanded under the historicopolitical circumstances of the times.

The origins of the estate council in Europe were twofold. Firstly, the incorporated market-cities, being separated from the political institutions of feudal-agrarian,

* *Standestaat* was the term employed by the German historians.

lordly-military political administration,* found themselves
without means of governing themselves.†

In their earliest period, they evolved a system of administration—a system of government by lot,‡ whereby
individuals selected by chance came together and formed
a council whose job it was to appoint and direct those
among the chosen members to act in the various capacities necessary to the administration of city affairs.

These early city councils were not unlike the clan
councils of agricultural and hunting times, excepting that
the extended family (clan) structure had been considerably reduced in size and significance, and that those
chosen for this council did not serve more than a year or
two, at which time another drawing was held and a new
set of amateur, temporary, part-time administrators was
chosen.

In due time government by lot proved unwieldy, and
professional politicans and administrators replaced the
amateur, part-time rulers, but the city council remained
the institution for governmental administration and the
electoral system remained as the procedure for the choos-
ing of administrative office-holders.

It was also the case that, as these market-cities (European and Greek) developed a wealthy upper stratum of
merchants (and occasionally artisan guild-masters), these

* *See* Chapter 3.

† Just as the Greek cities had after the Doric migrations separated
them from their kingly and priestly, clan-charismatic, political administrative structures.

‡ Just as had the Greeks in their earliest period of city-dwelling.

city patricians gained an influence in the city council far beyond their numerical strength. In fact, as the constituency of the councils passed from amateur to professional politicians, the *direct influence** of the rich became more pronounced than ever, for politicians, dependent upon their office for their wealth, became more and more easily manipulated by the upper classes.† In effect, then, the city council became a patrician council, and eventually this was formalized by the restriction of membership on the council to those possessing certain qualifying means, so that only those who qualified, in this later period, by possession of wealth (defined by the particular city involved, but usually defined in terms of property, a status factor held over from clan-charismatic, knightly aristocratic days) were allowed to electioneer for a seat on the council.‡

Although these patrician representatives to the city council claimed to represent all their constituents from a given district, and by the new tradition were supposed to do so, yet they rarely did so, and this led to a situation in which the unrepresented lower classes were driven to the point of revolt against the self-seeking and political monopoly of the upper strata.

At a slightly later point, as the lower city classes became resentful of their now subordinate position—having been

---

* Their indirect influence was always felt on the councils.

† Weber stated a preference for wealthy politicians not dependent on office for livelihood as derived from these circumstances.

‡ This is the origin of restricted qualifications for office-holding still prevalent in a *de facto* way in most of the Western world.

fully excluded from representation on the originally open governing council—various revolutionary activities began.

In Greece these have been documented by Aristotle and Plato, in Italy by Machiavelli; in Europe and England the documentation is less well known, but Marx, Weber, and others—especially the German historians, have done so. In Europe, as Weber has shown, the artisans, organized from ancient times into guilds, often asserted themselves through the guilds in this fashion. The situation could become highly complex with cross-class alliances and superartisan guilds and parties emerging (in alliance with wealthy merchant patrician families presently out of power and off the council).

Thus one can see that though the city council, as governing institution of the separated statelike cities, remained stable as an *institution,* the composition of those seated on that council was constantly contested and in flux. The view of liberal historians, that this institution mitigated against open violence—a view derived from the air of compromise developed during the estate-state period in Europe—is not at all accurate, but limited only to the historical point at which this institution, the city council, became the estate council, and was extended from the cities into the new territorial unit being united under the centralizing kingship.*

Here, we should only note that the city council re-

---

* Other instances of open violence exist of course—France, from 1750 to 1850, England, from 1620 to 1680, and Holland, from 1550 to 1600.

mained as an institution of government in the European and Spanish cities, although its composition was altered and altered again. And in the estate-state period of post-feudal Europe, this institution, carried by the city classes as one of their integral institutions, became the basis for the institution that was to emerge as the arena of compromise in that stalemated period.

Secondly, it was also true that from very ancient times, the knightly military class (of Europe and elsewhere, but Europe is specified here) had held courtly councils of allied clans (presided over by the head of the aristocratic clan headmen—the king—and attended by the head of each allied aristocratic clan—the military nobles).

This was a far more ancient institution than the city councils, existing in Europe (and elsewhere) as far back as the late hunting period, and revived in Europe after the fall of Rome as an integral part of the military and political maintenance of the upper strata of feudal society.

These two institutions, the city council and the council of military aristocrats were merged during the estate-state period of Europe (twelfth and thirteenth centuries). The estate councils, the unique political institution produced by Europe, were convened every few years at varying locations and attended by representatives of the landed feudal lords of the countryside and by representatives of the wealthy merchants and artisans of the cities, and by the regional king of the particular territory involved. (In Europe, as opposed to Greece, the lower city classes rarely unseated the wealthy patricians since the

burgeoning of early capitalist and precapitalist post-
Crusade commerce gave them great power. Even more
crucially, they had an ally in the kingship in its struggle to
consolidate its power. *And* most crucially, clan charisma
and aristocratic status were not yet broken since the
knights still were powerful in the countryside—neither of
the latter two factors were true in the fully separated
Greek city-state situation.)

These estate councils were known by various names:
Parliament in England, Estates General in France, and
Cortes in Spain.

THE PARLIAMENTS IN SPAIN AND LATIN AMERICA

In Spain, following the Moslem tradition of using the
cities as capital seats for political administration, these
estate councils or parliaments, called the *Cortes*, were
always held at the regional capital city of a given kingship's politically defined region. (This was similar to
Northern Europe where the estate councils were originally
held in the cities, but later on in Northern Europe they
were moved to neutral territory, often just outside of the
cities.)

Since no unified kingship emerged in Spain for many
centuries, there emerged a tradition of regionally distinct
parliaments convened in each of the regionally distinct
kingly domains.

The main regions were Aragon, Castile, and Portugal
(and later the southern regions, when brought under

Spanish control). In each region existed separate parliaments. There never was a superordinate single national parliament in Spain as there was in France and England. Since no total regional amalgam ever occurred in Spain, no single parliament ever became a fully national parliament. But the parliaments of Castile and Aragon and Portugal and the other provinces—convened at their various capital sites—acted as national parliaments at least within each province, and the effect and structure were the same as elsewhere. (Except that the city classes had more difficulty asserting their class interests on a broad scale, and a fully unified state or political action pattern was more difficult to attain for the kingship, although Charles V and Philip II did overcome this handicap after Isabella and Ferdinand laid the groundwork for at least partial unification; Portugal, due to knightly intransigence* and British foreign policy, was never brought together with the other two major Spanish provinces.)

This pattern of regional parliaments convened at regional capital cities with no totally unified governmental seat—kingly or parliamentary—was carried over to Latin America.

In the first instance, it was carried simply as part of the

---

* The Spanish knights made their last stand against kingly and merchant encroachments in Portugal. They fled from the other two provinces during the reign of Ferdinand and Isabella, and even an Iberian civil war could not bring them back. The civil war was lost by Ferdinand and Isabella, already overextended in the south of Spain (against the Moslems) and in Europe. Portugal, with the help of England, never returned to the fold.

Spanish national tradition of regional division and regional kingly and parliamentary separation. In the second instance, this kind of regional separation was exacerbated by the vast area of colonization and the incredible physical barriers existent between the various colonial regions. From Texas to Cape Horn is an unbelievably enormous land area. No single administration could have encompassed this, especially in the days of slow transportation and communications. On top of this, the South American land mass is one of the most inaccessible land areas of the world. The central American and Amazon jungles and the Andean mountains form impenetrable barriers of isolation. Even today air travel is the only connecting link between many of the regions of Latin America.

Therefore, because of tradition and necessity and the natural impediments of the land area, the system of separated, regionally distinct political and jurisdictional districts was reproduced in Latin America.

Regionally distinct, viceroyalty surrogate kingship districts were created by the Spanish crown. The surrogate kings took up governing residencies, with a courtly and priestly and bureaucratic entourage from Spain, in the capital cities of each of the early major regions. The Indies (at Havana), Mexico (at Mexico City), the Inca empire area (at Lima, since Cuzco was uninhabitable by Europeans due to its climate, and inaccessible to the sea due to its altitude), and Brazil (at Rio de Janeiro) formed the regional areas of kingly jurisdiction in the early days of colonization.

In each of these capital cities, according to Iberian precedent, tradition, and ongoing social structure, a parliamentary council was convened. As in Spain, the military landed lords and the upper priesthood were invited to sit on the council and also, according to the postfeudal precedent of all Europe and Spain, the city-dwellers without land—the "citizens"* (*vecinos*)—were also asked to elect representatives from their midst to attend the council.

In this manner, the estate council became a permanent institutional form there. The council was made up of all the upper strata acting for themselves, but also in the name of their respective city and country lower classes as in Europe, plus the Spanish viceroy (as a separate estate representing the Spanish kingly bureaucratic state according to European precedent derived from the compromises of the estate-state period). Thus, the estate council or parliament—called *Cabildo* in Latin America—was re-created and permanently convened in all the regional capital cities of Latin America.

In those regions colonized later where no viceroyal seat had been established by the Spanish kingship, the parliaments were organized and permanently institutionalized

---

* It is appropriate here to consider the origins in Greece and Europe of the word citizen—it originally meant merely "city-dweller," then it came to mean "participant in political affairs" when government by lot and election stipulated that all "accredited" city-dwellers must help in the governing of the city. Accreditation of citizenship, of course, led to the exclusion of foreigners and newcomers, and later of the poor. This latter measure ushered in the revolutionary era.

anyway, and local governors were appointed by the Spanish kingship as their permanent representatives to those councils so that the same political structure was extended to every local capital city of every province of Latin America whether part of the original major viceroyal districts or not.

REPRESENTATION ON THE REGIONAL PARLIAMENTS ("CABILDOS")

In early postfeudal Europe, the estate councils or parliaments were attended only by members of the upper classes, who were supposed to act in behalf of their negatively statused constituents. The manorial lords were supposed to represent the serf-peasants; the rich city merchants the artisans and free laborers; the merchant-gentry* the free farmers. In Latin America the free farmers, or *rancheros* (holders of *caballerías* or *peonías*), were represented by the estate lords, since no merchant-gentry existed in Latin America until the nineteenth century—at which time they did begin to make common cause with the ranchero free farmers.

Now, the constituency of the parliaments is especially crucial for Latin American history because, though the constituency of many—though not all—European parliaments was altered with the emergence of industrial capi-

---

* City patricians who bought land, titles, and servants, and resided in the countryside (often engaging in more efficient agricultural production than the subsistence-oriented knights and more successfully competing with them in commercial crop production).

talism and its new classes and class balance, the constituency of the Latin American parliaments became
frozen until the mid-twentieth century. In many of the
countries the parliaments remain unchanged to this day.*

It should also be remembered that *the constituency of
the Spanish parliaments,* after the kingly centralization
and Inquisition, *resembled more closely that of the
rapidly commercializing, centralizing states of Europe
than the Latin American constituencies ever did because
of:*

(1) The revival of *semi-feudalism* in the New World and
the subsequent re-emergence of a *knightly landed class.*

(2) The successful monopolization of all major economic
transactions by the Spanish kingship for three full centuries and the subsequent usurpation by England and the
United States of America as well as other nations of all
later major economic transactions, which created a situation where the commercial classes of Latin America never
ascended to prominence as did those of Europe and
America, and therefore, though seated on the parliamentary council, never had either the prestige, economic
power, or political independence of their European
counterparts.†

Thus, the Latin American parliaments resembled in

---

* In Colombia and Peru especially (though Peru has undergone some
change in recent years).
† The ramifications of this are discussed in Chapter 22.

constituency, style, and power balance the European parliaments of the earliest postfeudal estate-state period, where the knightly lords of the manors, controlling powerful serf-armies, arrogantly dominated the weak and diffuse kingly centralized state with its lack of funds and weak, barely professional army, and where they contemptuously dictated the terms of status, style, and protocol to the as yet politically weak, militarily insecure, and economically struggling commercial city classes.

The estate council of fourteenth-century Europe was reconvened in sixteenth-century Latin America. For the rush to America from semi-feudal sixteenth-century Spain was different from that emanating from commercial seventeenth-century England, France, and Holland. It was a rush to re-create the knightly style of life, not to accumulate monetary wealth. "Every man an *hidalgo*," the cry that was dying in sixteenth-century postinquisition, kingly centralized, commercializing Spain, echoed again in the mountains and across the plains of Latin America.

Adventurers flooded the New World from Spain, to re-create the Old. Land, servants, and titles, a style of life just beginning to die in Europe, lived again in full bloom on the new continent, and the dominant class of such a social structure lived on also and dominated the parliamentary councils of Latin America as arrogantly and as contemptuously as they had in the days when the knightly orders united to defend their position against the encroachments of the kings and merchants in fourteenth-century postfeudal Europe.

21

EARLY CLASS DISTINCTIONS AMONG THE SPANISH CONQUERORS

Not all the Spaniards acquired estates in the New World. "There were not enough *encomiendas* to go around. Only those who stood highest in the favor of the leader or had the strongest claim to rewards for distinguished service could hope for such grants."[1]

In Chile, for example, "in 1655 it was said that there were but two hundred who held *encomiendas*, whereas the total number of Spaniards must have been at least double that."[2] Thus a class of Spaniards without lands or serfs grew up in and around the cities in hope of someday receiving a land grant or being able to purchase or somehow acquire an estate.

Those who had received no Indian serfs or estates, and who had remained city-bound and landless, were known simply as "citizens," *vecinos*,* as distinguished from the lords (*encomenderos*) of the private serf-worked estates. *These two groups were rather sharply differentiated.*

---

* Landless, yet eligible for political office and parliamentary office as opposed to the serfs. The designation was derived from the postfeudal European market-cities where "citizen" meant legally free from serf-bond, and politically eligible for office-holding.

In the regional parliament (*Cabildo*) convened at Santiago, as in all Latin American cities, *"each group had its own representatives, the one being served by the minister of citizens (alcalde de vecinos), the other by a minister of lords (alcalde de encomenderos)."*[3] Following the traditional early parliamentary pattern of Spain, France, and England, the two contending classes formed into two parties and had two separate leaders on the parliamentary council. The two classes acted as separate "estates," the one landless, city-bound, and commercial, the other landed, country-oriented (at least in the very early period), and feudal.

"The former class occupied a decidedly inferior position in the colony. They enjoyed less social distinction, had no retinue of native attendants at their command, possessed no assured means of livelihood, and as yet had been given no opportunity to establish themselves on the land, except on a small scale as holders of urban lots and suburban *chacaras* (little estates just outside the cities aping the great estates of the *encomenderos**). They scarcely figured as masters in the country they had helped to conquer,"[4] and this festered in their "everyman-an-*hidalgo*" consciousness as an insult someday to be righted. Land, status, and power must be theirs, or they would remain in their own minds as nothing, as ridiculed. . . .

This class division is the basis for the now well-known

---

* The urban and suburban lots would soon be crucial when the luxuriating of the cities began, but as yet were the useless holdings of a weak, low-status, city commercial class.

two-party structure of the Latin American parliaments which in the postindependence period came to be known as the split between the *"liberal"* (landless, city commercial class) and the *"conservative"* (semi-feudal estate-lord class).

The intricacies of this political division among the upper strata (those eligible for seats on the parliament), and the involvement of the lower disenfranchised classes in this split, forms part of the framework in which the political drama of the postindependence period was played out.[5]

THE OBSESSION OF THE LANDLESS CLASS AND THE DOMINANT STATUS OF THE KNIGHTLY STYLE OF LIFE

As to the Spanish-descended landless citizens of the Latin American cities, *their continuing dream was someday to become an estate lord* and share the status, power, and style of life of that most exalted of Latin American classes. *To have land and servants and knightly political authority* was the obsession of the landless Spaniards. This was their reason for emigrating to the New World and this formed the thrust of their parliamentary politics.

They would bide their time in the cities trifling with commercial enterprises, the professions, and the lower echelon political and administrative offices, but these were merely means to the goal which was the estate, the serfs, and the status of the knight-on-horseback. For in Latin

America "everyone lives on distances. Scarcely anyone is where he is, but in advance of himself. And from *there* he governs and executes his life *here*. . . . Everyone lives as though his dreams of the future were already reality."[6]

And so in Latin America, though these landless Spaniards formed into an aggressive class of city commercial entrepreneurs, this was a class anticipatorially socialized into a different mold. It was a class-for-itself, but not a class-in-itself,* for it did not exist as a class merely with its own elective affinities (though these existed and were typical for this kind of class), but it also existed as a class with the elective affinities of the semi-feudal class grafted onto its own bursting forth to dominate its own affinities once the possibility of the primeval dreams' fullfillment appeared.†

This commercial city-bound class in Latin America fought the semi-feudal class savagely in contesting its political position and affirming its own, *but* at any period when the complete destruction and *total* defeat of the semi-feudal class seemed imminent, this class *sided with*

---

* A reversal of the old Marxian analysis of the capitalist proletariat.

† This was also the case in Europe in the early commercial period. The commercial classes bought estates and titles and aped the knightly aristocratic style of life—even married into this class whenever possible. But in England, France, and Holland, as opposed to Spain, Latin America, Germany, and East Europe, this class—the commercial class—and their elective affinities, emerged into full bloom as the machine created industrial capitalism from ancient merchant capitalism (as in the Weberian analysis). However, in Germany, East Europe, Spain, and Latin America the elective affinities of the commercial class (and the class itself) were always partially submerged beneath the knightly aristocratic class and elective affinities.

it and defended it passionately. For to annihilate this class and its style of life would be to annihilate the dream of land and servants and knightly status which was the primordial reason-for-existence of these landless, presently commercial Latin Americans.

Thus was an alliance born of the split. Thus were the bloody conflicts that were to occur belayed by the unity beneath. It is herein that lies the root of the confusion in the understanding of the Latin American commercial classes held by liberal historians. Moreover, this confusion was to become more complex yet, as the noncommercial, semi-feudal class became endowed with a steady capital supply in the cash-crop period that was to follow.

THE CONTROL OF THE CITIES: THE PARLIAMENTS, THE CITY OFFICES, THE CITY LANDS

Each regional district was governed at the top by the Spanish viceroyal governorship under the authority of the Spanish monarchy. But beneath these surrogate kingships and their courtly entourages in each regional capital, there was created, as mentioned, in the fashion of the Spanish cities, an estate council or parliamentary council made up of representatives from the jurisdictional districts within that territorial unit. In the manner of the Spanish regional parliaments, these councils met in the capital city, the largest city of the region.

The representatives consisted of the estate lord of each

estate within the region under question (or the greatest
estate lord representing a number of lesser lords), and
representing also the *caballería* and *peonía* small holders
(rancheros), who, whether they liked it or not, could not
sit on the council.*

Also seated on these regional parliamentary councils
were representatives from the city itself and often representatives from other lesser cities where local city councils
existed, but where no real regional estate council did.
Often members of the larger cities sat on behalf of those
from smaller ones.†

The representatives from the cities were the wealthiest,
most prestigious members of the landless commercial
class, *a sort of city patriciate,* but with much less status
than the estate lords, and in Latin America, with much
less wealth than their counterparts in Spain, England, or
Europe.

The two classes, as mentioned, actually had not only
"their own representatives" who acted as two separate
"parties," but they also had two different presiding min-
isters, a "minister of nonlanded citizens and a minister of
estate lords." The interests of the two classes were quite
different though their goals were ultimately the same.

The estate lords, through their much higher social
status and through the power of their serf-armies in the

---

* Just as the English upper gentry represented the yeoman (serfless
free farmers) and the lesser gentry, who could not be seated on the
council.
† This also was the precedent in Spain, England, and most of Europe.

countryside, came to dominate these regional (soon to be national) parliamentary councils. Their main interest in dominating these councils was almost identical to that of the Spanish and European knightly class when it dominated the estate councils, that is, to control and direct the land distribution system, to limit land grants to their class wherever possible, to inhibit the breakup of any landed estates, to limit all taxation and other governmental obligations attached to land tenure, and finally, to prevent all encroachments upon the civic, judicial, political, military, religious, and social authority of the estate owner.

The estate owners sought to monopolize, close off, and maintain all their rights to the land, and to inhibit any supranational control over their estates. *This all amounted to a negative, status quo kind of politics, for the estate lords had learned from inquisitional Spain that any compromise could lead to the long-term slow decay of their power and their authority.*

The rigid position they took in terms of protecting their privilege, a position they still hold today wherever they exist, is a position grounded in the historical knowledge of the erosion of lordly land rights and the disappearance of the landed class as a class. This they had just seen in Spain. They saw it again in the French Revolution, and have since then remained rigid in their unyielding position on economic, political, or civic encroachments upon their fief-rights, using every method—civic, military, criminal, political, religious—to maintain their position throughout history.

The estate lords succeeded in controlling the parliaments and completely controlling the land policies, which were made in the parliaments by consent of the Spanish kingship, right up through the independence period.

Thus, in the centuries preceding independence, the city-bound landless citizens had to content themselves with their landless existence and find other ways in which to enhance their status and power. There were two ways open to these landless citizens to enhance their power (their status could only be enhanced through the acquisition of a landed estate).

Firstly, they could control the offices of the cities, for the estate lords in the early period of colonization were too busy controlling, distributing, and establishing, extending, protecting, and making heritable, the great estates to have time or interest in the affairs of the as yet nonluxurious frontier cities. Thus the landless city-bound class came by default to control the offices of administration of the cities and all *local* political and civic affairs.

Although the kingship, through its civic viceroyalties and priestly bureaucrats, controlled the total administration of the territories, the estate lords eventually came to control the regional districts as representatives to the regional parliamentary councils while city officials came to control the affairs of the city. Later, in a further extension of their power, these city officers also came to control the lower bureaucratic offices of the surrogate kingly state structure, again by default of any other available personnel. The viceroyalty and priesthood controlled major policy decisions as direct representatives of the Spanish kingship, but the indigenous officials made most of the smaller decisions and carried out what they chose of the larger ones, ignoring what they chose to ignore as well, so that by the time of the wars of independence, the vice-royalties were almost honorific offices rather than actual administrative institutions, and the landless city class had extended its political power considerably.

In this fashion the city classes came to control the city offices and through them the cities' affairs. They also came to have great autonomy in policy-making since neither the Spanish surrogate kingships nor the indigenous estate lords knew or cared about the affairs of the cities in the early colonial period.

A second way in which the men of the city could expand their power was through commercial investments and enterprises. Here they encountered a major block, however, for mining, shipping, and all trade were controlled by the Spanish kingship under a total monopoly. The king's "Department of the Indies" implemented economic control and made all policy decisions. Besides this, all profits that were not taken by the kingship were taken by the estate lords, who controlled and directed most of the serf-produced mineral and agricultural products. Since serf labor was the only labor available in the early period, the estate lords naturally monopolized any major economic projects. So trade, mining, and agricultural production on a large scale were closed off to the serfless city classes.

Even large-scale businesses based on luxury items were impossible to enter since the estate lords, who would desire such luxuries, could import them from Europe through the monopoly middleman agency of the Spanish kingship, so that neither production of such items (since they were produced more cheaply abroad), nor distribution of those items (since the Spanish Department of the Indies controlled this) was open to the enterprising businessman.

The foregoing reason explains why the city classes were in the forefront in the struggle for independence; another was their desire to open up crown and church lands to colonization so that they could buy estates and become part of the high-status estate-lord class. These two reasons for demanding independence, interestingly, show the major conflict of interest which this class exhibits throughout its history. On the one hand, they desired independence to increase their commercial business possibilities, on the other, to leave the commercial realm behind and join the world of the lords and the servants and the land.

Commercially, then, only small business enterprises were available to the city-dwellers, and these they engaged in with much vigor and economic success, though status enhancement and personal satisfaction were not forthcoming for them even if such enterprises were successful.

There was one area of commercial investment, however, that was open to the landless class of Spanish conquerors, and which had a twofold attraction for them. That is, the city lands themselves.

It will be remembered that the Spanish cities, like the Italian and Greek city-states, owned quite a bit of land

surrounding them. This land was held in common by all
the citizens of that city and could be used only by them.

The administration of this land was, of course, in the
hands of the city officials. Thus the landless class, now in
control of the city offices, could also control the common
lands of the cities. This they did, first, by building little
suburban estates for themselves in and around the cities
to try and obtain some of the estate-lord's charisma; and
second, by coming to control all city lots so that any
construction thereon would bring them great profit and
financial control. The latter element became crucial, as
we shall see in Chapter 22, when the expansion of the
cities began and the estate-lords began to look for permanent luxury *city* accommodations.

These city lots became crucial as the colonial era ma-
tured, for when the estate-lords later began to move into
the cities a demand was created for luxury accommodation and places of amusement and recreation. This demand sent the value of the city lands soaring, and those in
economic and *political* control of these lands, through the
control of city offices and policies, were in an excellent
position to exploit the new conditions into economic and
political profit for themselves. For the representatives of
the cities had to be listened to now on the parliamentary
council when affairs of the cities were being considered,
since they had both the expertise and the actual control
over these affairs, *and for the first time, the affairs of the
cities were crucial to the estate-lords and to the development of the entire territory generally.*

The control of land in and near the cities, and the

political and administrative control of these lands as well
as the commercial control, *gave the city class its first power
base,* and its voice in the parliamentary councils became
greater, its expectations were raised and its bid for power
became more serious.

*But the very basis of their power was to be the chal-
lenge of their power. For the ascendancy of the city class
depended on the control of city lands, and this control
became most important at the point where the country-
bound estate class began to move to the cities*—just as the
Spanish lords had, and for similar reasons—and the city
plots were parlayed into luxury city houses. *All the power
and wealth acquired by this city class depended upon the
continuous movement into, and interest in, the cities
being newly exhibited by the estate-lords.** Yet the movement into the cities—in permanent or part-time residence
—and the naturally increased interest in city affairs subsequently shown by the estate-lords was the greatest threat
to the newly won and newly growing status and power of
the city class.

A Summary of Early Class Distinctions

Thus, though the parliamentary councils were dominated by the estate-lords, the city administration itself was
left to the landless Spaniards. For the *encomenderos* were
too busy controlling the dispensation and continuation of
land grants, and during this estate formation period, did

---

* The movement of the estate-lords to the cities will be analyzed in
Chapter 22.

not care about the administration of the still uninteresting cities. Even the Indian capital cities, having been stripped of their wealth and people, were, after their initial exotic quality wore off, not yet luxury centers by Spanish-Moslem standards.

The landless Spaniards, then, seeking political power and social position concomitant to their conqueror status, applied themselves with great enthusiasm and vigor to the one area left in which they could gain prestige, namely, the administration of the cities, (a) through occupancy of their offices, and (b) through control of their common lands.

In this way they developed (a) political investment in the cities' high offices—including positions as representatives in the regional councils meeting in their midst,* and (b) economic control of the lands of the city—an economic position which was at first spurious, but which came to be crucial when city land became necessary for luxury building as the estate-lords sought more permanent city accommodation (being attracted there, as we shall see, for political and social reasons).

---

* Though as a less privileged party, as the city merchants and merchant-gentry were in the English, German, French, Spanish, and all Northern European parliamentary councils. This situation mirrors closely the situation of all postfeudal Europe. The position of the commercial classes (largely city-bound, but slowly spreading to the countryside as agriculture became commercially exploitable) as a secondarily privileged class represented on the regional estate councils (or parliaments) was fully typical of all postfeudal Europe including Spain and Italy. This parallel should not be surprising, since the Spaniards carried these institutions with them and simply reconvened them on the new continent.

This subsequent movement to the cities by the estate-lords in the second century of Iberian domination, caused enormous political and social alterations in the Latin American social structure, both in the countryside and in the cities. Though this movement was at first hailed by the city classes, due to its financial benefits, it came to cause great trepidation in that class when the *permanent, vested* nature of this settlement became evident. Originally, the lords had always come to the cities for part of the year, then they slowly began to take up permanent residence, residing on their country estates only during holidays.

The permanent movement of the estate-lords to the cities re-created the very same situation which had occurred in reconquest, post-Moslem Spain.* That is, (a) political confrontation in the cities between the *knightly feudal* estate-lords and the *commercial* city patricians, with its concomitant intrigue, violence, and partial anarchy; and (b) anarchy in the countryside, due to the permanent withdrawal of the lord and his family to the city, with subsequent banditry, armed conflicts, and quixotic, heroic peasant uprisings.

These conditions were remarkably similar to those of reconquest Spain before the consolidation of the kingship. *But in Latin America these events were followed by no such consolidation and pacification, but rather by a quarter century of increased warfare and anarchy* in the

---

* Similar to the situation in Renaissance Italy, after the fall of the Holy Roman Empire.

movement of the colonies for independence from the Spanish kingly bureaucratic state.*

* It should also be noted that the conflict between the two upper strata did not erupt into actual total violence until the Spanish kingship with its reifying authority structure was permanently removed—first temporarily by Napoleon's invasion of Spain and his subsequent dethroning of the Spanish monarch, and secondly, and permanently, by the wars of independence.

22

THE LORDS OF THE SEMI-FEUDAL ESTATES MOVE TO THE GROWING LUXURY OF THE CITIES

Beginning in the late colonial period, around the second century of Iberian occupation, the lords of the semi-feudal estates began to follow the pattern of urbanization which had been established in Spain.

The reader will remember that the Spanish knights, seeing before them the great treasures and luxuries of the Moslem capital cities, did not remain content on their country estates but were drawn to these great pleasure domes, as opposed to the Northern European knights, who, faced with no temptations from the austere, dull, commercial market-cities of the northern areas, remained on their feudal estates—at least until the seventeenth century.*

* After the seventeenth century when increased trade, prosperity, and the expansion of the kingly court made the cities more interesting, the North European knights moved there. But they never were involved in the affairs of the city the way the Spanish and Italian knights were, although in the nineteenth century they did play such a role, but their power was reduced by then.

Thus the Spanish knights, unlike those of Northern Europe, quickly became a class of city-dwelling, absentee landowners, desirous of the luxuries and splendor of the great capital cities left by the Moslems, and deeply involved in the political life of the cities.

The first cities in Latin America to be rebuilt as luxury centers were those that served as viceroyal seats for the surrogate kingship and their courtly entourages. In Mexico and Peru,* where Indian treasure and luxury palaces had existed, the process of re-luxuriating in the Spanish style began early, as these were the two major seats of kingly authority in the New World and the viceroyal governors demanded quarters befitting a king and his court.

The Spanish Americans, in the hope of gaining political or economic rewards, were anxious to please the king and his representatives, and anxious also to re-create some of the aristocratic elegance of the Spanish court in order to enhance their status and remove the air of provinciality and rusticity that inevitably hung over the colonies in the early years. Therefore, they began to build courtly accommodations for the surrogate kings.

Since the estate-lords cherished the social prestige and luxury surrounding the viceroys and their entourages, and also because it was politically expedient and necessary to engage in courtly intrigue and to benefit from courtly

* Meaning the viceroyalty of Peru, that is, the boundaries of the Inca empire as they originally stood, including Bolivia, Ecuador, North Chile, and Peru.

largess, they began to spend more time in these capital seats, from political necessity and for social pleasure.

Since the lords were spending longer periods of time in these cities, they soon came to demand better and more luxurious accommodations for themselves—accommodations equaling those afforded to the Spanish viceroys, bureaucratic priests, and other kingly functionaries. With these luxuries, the city class, who controlled the city real-estate plots, were glad to provide them.

The city class, as mentioned, saw this as their first chance to gain wealth and power, a prospect that spurred them to the task of organizing, building, embellishing, and renting newly created living quarters for the estate lords who had begun to demand such accommodations.

In this way the viceroyal seats of Spanish kingly authority in Latin America became the first luxury centers in the New World, and the estate-lords of these regions began to spend more and more of their time in these luxurious social and political centers.

It was not long before the lords of other regions farther from these capital centers began to cast a jealous eye toward the excitements, intrigues, and luxuries of the viceroyal centers. By comparison, their regional capital cities were nothing more than rustic frontier towns. Therefore, emanating from this jealousy, a competitive spirit arose among those estate-lords in the more distant regions of Latin America. A demand arose to refurbish and adorn the regional capitals, to make them fit for the aristocratic style of life demanded by the estate-lords of those regions, to make them as beautiful as the viceroyal centers.

Once again, as soon as this demand began, the city class of those regional capitals responded to the call, recognizing this as a chance to gain wealth and power just as their brethren at the viceroyal centers had.

Thus, in the same way as at the major capital cities, the then minor regional capitals became luxury centers in which the estate-lords spent more and more of their time, aping Spanish courtly ways. Simultaneously the regional parliaments convened at these regional capital cities assumed more of a politically significant role.

Havana, Lima, Mexico City (as viceroyal centers), and Santiago, Caracas, Bogotá, Buenos Aires, Rio de Janeiro (the Portuguese viceroyal center), Bahía, and other such cities grew rapidly.* They quickly grew splendid from the conqueror's plunder from the mines, purchase from abroad of all sorts of luxury items, and slave labor from within.

Thus, well before independence, the attraction of the cities as luxury centers was already drawing the estate-lords to their midst. It was not long before these country lords came to live full time in the cities and to be so absorbed by the cities' delights and the affairs of state that they began leaving the affairs of their estates to paid overseers and administrators.

---

* The nonviceroyal cities grew as regional capitals in the typically Iberian semi-feudal style as a legacy from the Moslem kingly capital cities with regional jurisdiction.

The Spanish kingship also had something to do with the lords moving in to the cities—just as it had in Spain.

The kingship, in its attempt to reduce the power of the estate-lords, "forbade the *encomendero* to live among his wards."[1] Legislation, whose (overt) purpose was to protect the Indians from abuse by the Spaniards, was enacted with the latent hope of reducing the power of the landed class, as this had occurred in Spain.

The idea was to bring the lords to the cities so that (a) they would come under the scrutiny of the surrogate kings, and (b) to buy them off and into the kingly bureaucratic state by bestowing high offices on them. (Later, offices were restricted to the Spanish-born only, when the loyalty of the colonists became suspect in the eyes of the Spanish state.)

Though this had worked in Spain, it did not work in Latin America, for the surrogate kingships had neither the power nor the authority of the Spanish kingship, but were almost captive honorific offices of the regional parliaments dominated by the estate-lords in the late colonial period.

The offices in Latin America were not well integrated into the Spanish kingly bureaucracy anyway, but actually had been coopted by the Latin American landless city class who now viewed with a jealous and angry eye the bestowal of these offices upon the lords.

Paradoxically, instead of weakening the estate-lords, the Spanish kingships helped provoke a situation which was to cause tremendous class conflict, political chaos, and violence in the near future.

The city classes now had a third reason for desiring

separation from the Spanish kingly state added to their desire for economic independence and crown lands: that is, removal of royal and viceroyal control of offices so they could get them back from the estate-lords. These were offices over which they had formerly held control by default, since the lords had previously been uninterested in them during the early colonial period.

Thus from a very early period, the lords were induced by kingly decree to stay away from their estates. The *encomenderos* obeyed, not because of the power of the Spanish kingship, but because they were intrigued by the cities anyway.

The movement of the estate-lords into the developing cities had enormous ramifications for the future of the Latin American social and political structure. Both the structure of the countryside and that of the cities was violently and radically altered by this movement.* The social order of the countryside dissolved with the removal of the clan-charismatic estate-lords, for a serf will bend to a lord or a king, but not to a paid, plebeian administrator or overseer. The political balance in the cities and the regional parliaments was drastically altered as well; competition for city offices intensified, and all affairs of state were now under the scrutiny of the estate-lords. The city classes were placed in a precarious position, and their newly won wealth and power were directly threatened. This process put the entire sociopolitical structure of Latin America in flux.

* As it had been in Spain and Italy.

RAMIFICATIONS OF THE MOVEMENT OF THE ESTATE-LORDS TO THE CITIES

Part I: The Effect on the Countryside

The estate-lords and their families began spending most of each year in the largest regional city accessible to their estate (the city in which the regional parliament was convened and to which the estate lord was a representative).

This had profound effects both upon the cities in which they then resided and upon the semi-feudal countryside which they left. In the countryside, the exit of the lord left the rural territories without civil and military authority, therefore abandoning the serfs to a state of dereification from the clan-charismatic legitimacy symbols. In this manner a dangerously anarchic situation was created and began to prevail in the rural districts previously administered by, and legitimated by, the estate-lords and their charismatically invested family with its aristocratic heritage.

Slowly, the fruits of anarchy began to bloom in the Latin American countryside. The previously stable serf populations began to drift from the estates, dislocations and uprisings became more common. Banditry grew out of dislocation and dereification from authority. Disorder and rebellion grew from the absence of the authority figures on the estates and the subsequent takeover of power by figures who lacked the authority traditionally obeyed by the serf populations.

In the cities, the entrance of the estate-lords upset the political balance of those cities and set off a series of power struggles, where the landed feudal and landless commercial classes began competing with each other on an interclass basis, and where powerful aristocratic and patrician families began competing with one another for total control on an intraclass basis. This competition eventually led to such chaos and violence that an anarchic situation once more emerged where legitimacy was shattered and city populations dereified from authority symbols. Elements of naked force, in the form of professional soldiers, professional thieves, and professional politicians, were increasingly employed by the contending classes and families in their struggle to dominate the amorphous, anarchic political structure.

The Distintegration of Legitimacy in the Countryside

ABSENTEE LORDS AND MESTIZO OVERSEERS

The estate-lords in Latin America had always spent part of the year in the cities—as representatives to the parliaments, or as seekers of some political or social gain at the viceroyal court, or as purchasers of some luxury items from abroad at the nearest port or port-connected city.

Being away from the estate for many months at a time, the estate-lord's natural response "was to employ an overseer"[2] to care for the affairs of the estate. "This individual was most commonly drawn from the class of mestizos (half-breeds) which grew up rapidly in the colonies."³

As described previously, the mestizos were in a difficult social position, for they could neither attain Spanish lordly status, nor accept Indian serfdom. Therefore, the overseer position had special appeal for them since they could at once assume some of the authority of the Spanish lords and at the same time could stand above the Indians in status and order them around. They felt this was their right. The overseer position was a position halfway between the lord and the serf, the Spaniard and the Indian. A more fitting role for the mestizos could not have been invented.

For this reason, those mestizos who could, found positions as overseers on the great estates, and while the lords were away, were invested with the authority of the lord. However, the mestizos, as we have mentioned, disidentified with the Indian serfs. The emergent overseers resented them as a symbol of what they were trying to break away from. Because of this, the mestizos hated and looked down upon the Indian serfs, and as overseers, generally, treated them more cruelly, more mercilessly, than the estate-lords who could afford to be beneficent in the knightly style. The overseers made the serfs work harder and longer than the lords, and doled out heavier punishments for intransigence.

The Indian serfs, for their part, tended to direct their status resentment toward the overseers rather than the absentee lords. In fact, the absentee lords often became idealized from afar as saviors who would return each year and ameliorate the hardships inflicted upon the Indians by the cruel overseers. Ironically, since the lords began visiting their estates only on holidays and summer vacations, they *did* begin to play this role! When the lords returned, it was always holiday season, a time for celebrating; and the lords, feeling in a specially beneficent mood during these holiday seasons, and being able to be even more beneficent since they really cared little about the actual functioning of the estates so long as a certain minimum productivity was maintained, acted graciously and sympathetically toward the problems of the serfs.

The lords often brought gifts and verbal praise to his noble wards, the serfs, and they often rebuked the overseers, though doing little to stop their cruel practices and caring little about them in reality.

Almost imperceptibly a strange alteration of the legitimacy structure occurred in the Latin American countryside. *The actual legitimacy of the lord-serf relationship* began to break down as the lords spent less and less of their time on the estates but the dereification from lordly authority took a strange turn. That is, *as the serfs became dereified from the feudal authority structure, they began to direct their hostility, resentment, and rebellion against the overseers,* to rise up against them, to leave the estates entirely, or at least to obstruct work on the estates, or work as little as possible. And instead of directing hostility toward the *lords,* they instead began to idealize the lords as messianic saviors, noble *"men-on-horseback"* who would come back some day to right the wrongs which the cruel mestizo overseers were inflicting upon them. The Indians always considered the "man-on-horseback" as a God-like figure because the Spaniards were the first men they had ever seen on horseback—indeed they had never seen a horse before—and the Spaniards were considered to be God-figures when they first arrived on the continent. This explains why the "man-on-horseback" had special significance as part of the Indians' mythology from the point of the Spanish arrival onward.

The hero-on-horseback became the growing myth of the downtrodden, now dereified, serf, and this myth was added to the Indians' other myth of redemption, which was the return of their ancient clan lands, derived from the days when the Spaniards coopted the land of their communal villages and tenanted them on the great estates as landless serfs. These two myths fused, and the seething dream of the serf was the dream of the "man-on-horseback" who would return some day and lift the yoke of serfhood and forced labor, right the wrongs inflicted by the hated overseers, and restore the lands stolen by the now distantly recalled "foreign" conquerors. That the lords were the descendants of those who had taken their lands was temporarily forgotten.*

And so the lords were *not* hated, and they did *not* lose the loyalty of those serfs remaining on their estates, for the resentment was deflected and displaced onto the unnecessarily harsh and unsympathetic mestizo overseers.

* The Indian serfs had always harbored messianic redemption myths even in pre-Spanish times. This was typical in all urban-centered empires.

The lords remained venerated, becoming even more idealized than they had been when they actually exerted their power over the serfs in the days when they had resided upon their lands.

Since the lords had symbolized power and authority upon their estates, no superordinate authority existed above the estate-lords in Latin America to symbolize legitimacy for the system, beyond their person or their role. No kingship stood as unifying symbol above the lords, no vassalage hierarchy stood as umbrella under which legitimated authority could be localized, no bureaucratic structure of invested officeholders linked the system to its center. In short, no institution stood above or around the estate-lord himself as representative of legitimated authority.

The semi-feudalism inherited from the Spaniards and made more extreme in Latin America by the great geographic and social distance of the kingship provided for no central state structure, but was made up instead of private family estates, little empires upon which the civic, military, religious, political, social, and economic authority was invested in the lord and his family alone.

Given this social system, *the removal of the lord and his family from the estate meant the total removal of all visible signs of legitimacy and authority from that estate.* Thus the mestizo overseer, even if he didn't want to, and even if he wanted to be humane, was forced to use naked force against the serfs because the latter did not accept the authority of his person.

As the estate-lords spent less and less time upon the

estates, the overseers had to exert more and more naked force to exert their power, and the clan charisma of the lord became transferred to the myth of the benevolent hero-on-horseback, and the resentment of the serf population grew.

The Growing Anarchy of the Countryside

The movement of the estate-lords away from the countryside and the placing of nonlegitimated overseers in their stead set in motion two major trends.

Firstly, resentment was always part of the serf's consciousness, but usually it was self-directed as a rationalization for the negatively privileged status the serf found himself in, or else it was displaced upon strangers, whom the serfs mercilessly tortured and murdered, given the chance. It was never directed at the lords except in times of total social revolution, and then almost always only with the aid and direction of an independent, dissatisfied intellectual class. In Latin America this resentment grew cancerously under the yoke of the overseers who had to resort to greater and greater naked force to exert their power.

This resentment, as we shall see, became channeled into three different forms of anarchic activity which often were expressed in one mixture. It was expressed in (a) *banditry*, with a very high rate of unnecessary violence to the victims, (b) *warfare*, during the independence period,* and (c) *feuding*, especially the political inter-

* And afterward in national wars, and later in revolutionary movements.

and intraclass feuding of the postindependence period, which erupted into incredible violence all over the Latin American continent.*

All three of these forms of channeled resentment merged at varying times so that warfare and banditry and political activity were often almost indistinguishable. Because of the underlying resentment festering in the lower strata, the passion involved in all three spheres frequently far exceeded both the goals and the intentions of the original reasons for the actions.

Secondly, *dislocation* of populations began to occur.† There was a resumption of the terrible dislocations of people that had begun during the conquest period and had apparently been ended by the full establishment of the semi-feudal estates.

With the withdrawal of the lords began the slow withdrawal of some of the serfs. Young men especially began to drift to the hills and to the cities. The stream was extremely slow in the beginning, and these early drifters did not go far, for they were still largely dependent upon the estates for food and clothing since the cities were often too far away or as yet without economic opportunity.

The first "dislocated ones" therefore usually lived in the nearby hills, and came back to the estates to do odd chores, or to help at harvest and planting times in order to

---

* As in prerevolutionary Mexico. For a more typical situation, though the most extreme in all Latin America, "La Violencia" in Colombia is an example. See Vidich: "The Politics of Colombia," unpublished article, New School for Social Research.

† 1700–1800.

earn such necessities as food staples and clothing. They were often part-time peasants and part-time bandits. When they were not on the estates and were beyond the authority of the overseers and absentee lords, they spent their free time carousing, often drunk, around the hills and trails of the vicinity terrorizing those passing through. They were really amateur bandits out for the pleasure of dominating and frightening others, rather than for actual robbery, since they still earned much of their keep on the estate. However, the wars of independence increased the number of those dislocated a thousandfold, and created the fully professional, almost paramilitary bandits who attained political significance later on where they roamed the Latin American countryside. The kind of amateur, rowdy, sadistic, part-time banditry just described has continued throughout Latin American history. At this time also, these dislocated ones entered the cities only now and then for entertainment and thrills. Subsequently, at times during the postindependence period of the political feuds, these men often found employment as bodyguards for the absentee lords, as professional soldiers, and as professional thieves and assassins.

As the lordly clan charisma was removed, the authority of the serf clans was also weakened. Since the role of the serf in general was questioned, the status of the obedient serf fulfilling the role of father in the serf family was questioned by the younger family members. Young men and women began to question, rebel against, and leave the canopy of family authority.

In this context many of the serf women (as well as the young men) became dissatisfied with their lot as serfs, or with the men available on the estate. Adventurously they began to join those seemingly more exciting men in the hills *so that semipermanent, reproducing settlements* of these dislocated serfs and serf bandits began to grow up *as a permanent feature of the social structure.*

Often too, the more attractive of the serf girls on the estates were drawn off to the rich cities as entertainers, dancers, or prostitutes. Concubinage and prostitution had always been established as a line of upward mobility, even in Indian empire days. Thus women as well as men began *very slowly* to drift away from the rural estates.

The dislocations, then, increased the anarchic situation slowly developing in the countryside, and not only bandits but whole communities began to flourish outside of any legitimating authority structure.

This situation in the countryside never reached its logical fulfillment because the wars of independence intervened and absorbed the whole continent. The resentment, otherwise unfocused and random, was to be redirected temporarily at the Spanish crown, and the dislocation was to be utilized by the colonial upper classes as a blessed source of angry, willing, adventurous men to be tapped as soldiers. The entire process was thus channeled into something new.

Under these pressures, the processes begun in the countryside were not to abate. Instead they were exacerbated by the very wars which were temporarily to postpone them. As the war lingered on, the countryside was to become still more anarchic, and the dislocations were to increase one thousandfold as the battlefields changed hands again and again. The resentment was to remain, simmering, and the banditry was to become ever more violent and *far better organized*. The victory won by the upper-class colonials against the Spaniards was to be challenged by the myth that had been born on the lordless estates and had grown to manhood in the battles for independence, as heroes-on-horseback emerged, full-blooded, from the dust of the dead.

RAMIFICATIONS OF THE MOVEMENT OF THE ESTATE-LORDS TO THE CITIES

Part II: The Effect on the Cities

In the early colonial period the lords of the great *encomienda* estates were interested only in insuring and enhancing the status of their estates. They sat on the parliamentary councils convened in the regional capital cities once or twice each year, but were only interested in matters directly pertaining to their estates in one way or another.

But as their residence in the cities grew longer and more permanent, and as their status and estates became completely secured, their general political interests broadened, along with their extended social participation in the total society.

At the same time, in the early colonial period, the landless city class had inherited by default most of the supervision of the affairs of the cities, and also much of the general regional supervision, in their function as minor officials employed below the Spanish-born kingly appointed officials in the viceroyal bureaucratic state structure. Since much of the power and status of the landless citizens depended upon their control of these offices and affairs, they guarded them jealously against incursions by others, especially attempted incursions by mestizos, which at times were successful.

Now a major threat appeared to the landless Spanish citizens of the Latin American cities, for the estate-lords were becoming interested in the offices and policies of the cities and territorial regions.

In addition, the landless citizens, as representatives of the city classes to the parliamentary council, had coopted considerable political power in the absence of attempts by estate-lords to consolidate such control during the early colonial period, when the lords had remained rurally based most of the year.

But now the estate-lords were beginning to sit more permanently on, take more of an interest in, and call more frequently, the parliamentary councils. Moreover, they began to dominate not just matters pertaining to the land, but all matters, economic, political, and social, to the further exclusion of the landless city class.

Lastly, the kingship, in its attempt to control the estate-lords by drawing them off the land as it had successfully done in Spain, had begun to appoint the lords to high positions in its colonial bureaucratic state structure. This, too, angered and made jealous the city class which occupied the lower echelon officers and had never been appointed to the higher ones.

Thus the kingship's policy caused class conflict among the Latin American upper classes, since its policy strengthened rather than weakened the estate-lords. This policy also built up the political ambitions of the lords so that eventually they wanted access to *all* high bureaucratic offices at home, and began to demand independent and more representative appointment procedures. The early phases of the lords' split with the Spanish monarchy, which insisted upon appointing Spanish-born Spaniards to these high offices in order to insure their loyalty to Spanish kingly goals, had begun, and eventually they joined the landless city classes of Latin America in their drive for independence from Spanish kingly domination.

Two processes began as a result of the entrance of the estate-lords into the cities and their subsequent interest in all phases of the political, social, and economic life of the territory:

(1) A severe class rivalry developed between the landless city-dwelling citizens who had commercial interests and the now permanently city-dwelling estate-owning lords. This showed itself in every manner of political life, including the outward breach between the two estates or parties on the parliamentary council.

Conflicts between the commercial class and the landed class became more common and more intense. Real political rivalry occurred for the first time. The lower class would be drawn into this rivalry eventually, their resentment being redirected and made useful to the upper classes again, but in a different direction.

(2) A rivalry arose among the great lordly aristocratic families for control of offices, parliamentary seats, and all other affairs of state.

In Spain and Latin America, the structure of separated private estates resembling little empires created a tradition making each landed estate actually a family fief, in which the aristocratic family held total military, political, economic, social, and jurisdictional control over their serfs with no limitations placed upon their powers—there was not even a vassalage limitation. Thus holding total authority, the aristocratic families became accustomed to not having any limits placed on them.

Sharing power was unknown and uncongenial to them; political compromise was beyond their consciousness even where compromise would be more efficient than other methods.

Any political rival outside of the single particular family circle of the political participant was considered a total enemy to be dealt with as an outlaw, as an outsider, beyond the traditional bounds of authority of the particular family fief jurisdiction.

So powerful was family loyalty that no one outside the

aristocratic family circle was trusted, for no one could gain prestige and power except by marriage into an aristocratic estate-holding family, and power could only be extended through clan and clan-land expansion in the semi-feudal system.

Since these lordly families moved to the cities in their entirety, and established residence under one roof once more, it was quite natural that they maintained their previous reality and brought with them their governing tradition. And it follows from this that they tried to reproduce their condition of total control over affairs upon which they impinged.

In their previous estate world, if they could not get what they wanted legitimately, they took it by naked force, so that naked force and the step beyond the legitimate usage of power was always part of their habitual political style. This latter "tradition" of stepping beyond legitimate power boundaries and the subsequent institutionalization of open violence among the Latin American estate-holding classes was derived directly from the frontier nature of the settlement and its *conquistador*, personal power, tradition.*

This political style of the Latin American neo-knightly

*This anarchic, "beyond the law" tradition was eventually broken in the northern part of the United States, but was not broken where individual estate-owners, such as the cattle barons of the southwest and the plantation aristocrats of the south, held total authority over their lands, as in Latin America. In both these territories, naked violence for political ends still exists as an accepted, traditional technique of political actions. The vigilante spirit, preceded by open lawlessness and violence on the North American frontier as well, still persists in Texas and the southwestern cowboy-cattle country.

semi-feudal class was reproduced in the cities, first in its clash with the landless city commercial class, and second, in its clash with other families of its own class.

Violent rivalries arose between aristocratic clans meeting head-on in the new city environment and competing for the same political prizes. Competition for the top bureaucratic offices and parliamentary seats (previously decided by regional districting, but now less defined than before) became fierce. Extended face-to-face confrontations between the aristocratic families occurred for the first time, as the circle of the social world became smaller when it became city-centered. As social contact increased, political rivalry increased as well.

Thus the movement to the cities by the estate-lords broke the political balance of the old society, both between the city and the landed classes, and within the landed class itself.

Interclass and intraclass rivalries began to grow and become more and more complex, just as they had in Spain and Italy where the movement of the knights into the cities created a clash between them and the city-merchant patricians. This clash had led to violent feuding and century-long bloodshed in which anarchy prevailed and naked force emerged in its wake, with the purveyors of naked force gaining political power. Professional soldiers, thieves, assassins, and demagogues entered the open arena of feuding families and classes, to become an increasingly crucial factor as anarchy spread.

Just so was this process to be repeated in Latin America but not just yet . . . for in the century and a half before independence, the protective canopy of the Spanish kingship still spread over the continent of Latin America. Its viceroys and bureaucrats—civil and priestly —still held sway in the land and kept the antagonists apart.

Though distant from the countryside and providing no legitimating effect there, in the cities the viceroyal governors and their courts still held great prestige. They sat in the parliaments as the fourth estate, as the kings sat in the Spanish and European parliaments. They still commanded the highest authority in the land—and commanded, as well, the Spanish troops dispatched by the Spanish kingship for keeping order in the colonies. Therefore, though the rivalries of class and family conflict among the upper strata were on the verge of breaking, the anarchic situation was temporarily held in check by the still legitimate supreme authority in the land.

So powerful was the presence of the Spanish kingship and the symbolic authority vested in the viceroyalties, that no revolutionary challenge of its authority occurred until Napoleon's new citizens' army dethroned the Spanish kingship itself.* And, as long as the authority and legitimacy of the Spanish kingship were recognized in Latin America, the internal political conflicts remained subdued.

The movement toward independence itself, however, was generated by the subdued conflict in the upper strata. For it was the worsening position of the landless city class that provided the first impetus toward independence from

* An event that occurred after the North American Revolution.

Spanish authority. But it is still true that not until the monarchy was actually dethroned, did any real attempts at rebellion occur. And, it is even more true, that not until the estate-lords decided that separation from Spain was in their interest, did any *successful* rebellions occur.

THE LATIN AMERICAN CITIES RETAIN THE KNIGHTLY STYLE OF LIFE

The Estates as Symbolic Representations of Aristocratic Family Unity and Positively Privileged Status

Though it became the case that most of the estate owners and their families lived in the cities during most of the year, the "great house" on the estate and the estate itself *became even more venerated then before, for they became the symbol of family unity, loyalty, and aristocracy.*

The aristocratic families, in an attempt to maintain their positively privileged status, which in Latin America was based solely on estate possession, worked hard to maintain the invidious distinction of estate-holding. With conspicuous ceremonial display and fanfare, they retired to their estates on holidays and during the summer months, when the cities got unbearably warm. While in the cities, they talked endlessly of the great leisure times they spent on their estates with their "noble wards"* and their magnificent steeds. The estate-lords always main-

---

* Even now one hears of noble peasants (*Jibaros* in Puerto Rico, *Inquilinos* in Chile)—of course, they are considered subhuman once they actually enter the cities.

tained that their "true home" was the estate. The cities, though actually preferred for their excitement, intrigue, *and comforts*, were always considered crude, commercial, and common.

In this way, given the past history of Latin America as a society where status was always linked with land and where the city landless classes longed for the day when they too could gain land and the status that went with it, the estate-lords *successfully maintained* their clan-charismatic legitimacy. The system of status based on holding landed estates was not only maintained but *intensified*, for now one did not even have to move to the countryside to assume lordly status; all one had to do was somehow acquire an estate and stock it with servants and maintain it for its symbolic rather than its political or economic value.

This latter circumstance caused the landless class to venerate even more the lordly values and styles, since entrance into this upper stratum seemed more possible than ever. As a result, the landless city class came even more than before under the spell of the status affinities of the landholding semi-feudal class and copied even more closely the style of life and aspirations of that class, and their own commercial elective affinities became even further buried beneath their ever-growing dreams of semi-feudal grandeur.

The acceptance of the status myths of the semi-feudal class by the landless city class further encouraged the tendency in the aristocratic class to maintain its symbols of legitimacy which otherwise might have slowly been eroded in the new city milleu.* Through conspicuous consumption they kept the values of their estates high, and maintained the invidious comparison which they might have lost had the commercial classes not been caught up in their spell†

Thus did the lordly families successfully maintain their position as the most positively privileged status group. Thus also was the aristocratic style of life maintained in Latin America and carried to the cities, there to become abstracted, mythologized, and made an even more potent symbol to those living it and to those desiring to live it . . .

This style of life in all its aspects far outlasted the social conditions which engendered it, due to a set of peculiar and anomalistic conditions arising out of Latin America's unique historical sequences.

Meanwhile, although now city-based, the estate-lords maintained intact their status, their style of life, and their family unit. They, and everyone else in Latin America, came to look upon their holdings as "ancestral estates" to

---

* The knightly elective affinities and styles were slowly eroded in France, England, and Holland, where the elective affinities of the commercial city classes came slowly to dominate the knightly ones. Eventually, even in the countryside, commercial values replaced knightly values.

† It should be kept in mind also that in Latin America the commercial city classes never gained the monetary success of their counterparts in England, France and Holland, while the neo-knightly class gained an unprecedented capital source of its own from cash crops and other raw materials which its European counterparts never achieved.

be prized as symbols of the social stratum to which they and their families belonged. Each year, the *entire extended family group* would "gather on their paternal estates and renew and strengthen their kinship ties."[4] These yearly contacts served both to maintain their invidious distinction over the landless classes, and to preserve the solidarity and blood-bond of the particular family unit involved.

This practice continued both the landed aristocratic tradition generally, and also the tradition of *clan loyalty*.

From the earliest days, through three centuries of Spanish colonial history and even through one hundred years of independence, the mark of the semi-feudal estates on the national life may be seen. Both rural and urban life have been fashioned out of estate-holding. "The social class to which one belongs depends mainly upon one's relationship to the land-holding class. One's place in the body politic itself is founded upon the same factor . . ."[5]

 PART **IV**

The Spanish Kingly State Structure in the Latin American Colonies

23

THE STRUCTURE OF SPANISH KINGLY AUTHORITY ON THE NEW CONTINENT: THE VICEROYS

In principle, the Spanish kingship, through its bureaucratic council of the Indies, controlled all colonial affairs, military, religious, economic, and, of course, political.

"The major senior functionaries in the Americas were the viceroys"[1] (literally, sub-kings). Actual surrogate kingly-bureaucratic courts were set up at what were then the regional capitals of the newly conquered territories.

There were three main viceroyalty districts in Latin America. "The viceroy of 'New Spain' held court in Mexico, with jurisdiction over the whole of middle America. The viceroy of Peru operated even more magnificently from Lima, nominally controlling almost the whole of Spanish South America, over the Andean cordillera as far as the Rio de la Plata and Patagonia."[2]

"As Spain's responsibilities in the Americas increased, it became necessary to provide additional centres of government. The viceroyalty of 'New Granada'—with jurisdiction over the northern part of South America—was created in 1717; but it was not until 1776 that the Rio de la Plata was removed from the dominion of Peru. Lesser divisions (captaincies-general) were formed in Guatemala, Venezuela, Cuba, and Chile."[3]

Thus, each of the regional capitals, even if they had no viceroy, had at least a local representative of the kingship, and each of these "captaincies-general" had with him at least a small bureaucratic (priestly as well as civil) courtly entourage from Spain.

So, the presence of the kingship was felt in all parts of the Latin American Continent, though in the more remote parts it was felt later and with somewhat less prestige, and surrounded by considerably less courtly pomp. The Spanish kingship spread its mantle of legitimacy over the land. Its authority was supreme and unquestioned—if its power was often lacking—and it lent an aura of stability to the already appearing anarchic tendencies that were festering in the colonial womb.

The surrogate kings and their courtly bureaucratic entourage symbolized the Spanish kingship and formed the only nucleus around which all of the contending classes in Latin America could defer. In this way they promoted stability and were able to maintain a semblance of unity in the New World. But the cloak of Spanish kingly authority was to be suddenly removed by historical events outside of the colonial world, and the process of dereification from Spanish kingly authority—which was very slowly occurring (especially amongst the landless commercial city class)—was to be hastened beyond all expectation, and the course of Latin American history violently altered in the process. But we are ahead of ourselves. . . .

THE BUREAUCRATIC ENTOURAGE OF THE SURROGATE KINGSHIP

Below the kingly appointed governors was a bureaucratic state structure—not unlike that of the Spanish one, but far less differentiated—the main body of which was the council for Latin American affairs, modeled after the Council of Justice of Spain (*audiencia*—high court of justice—the most supreme bureaucratic department of state under the Spanish structure).

This highest bureaucratic department of state, like the viceroyalty, was composed exclusively of Spaniards born in Spain and appointed by the Spanish kingship. They were chosen primarily for their showing of loyalty to the Spanish kingship.

The Spanish kingship refused ever to appoint anyone from the colonies, feeling—and quite correctly so—that the interests of the colonials would inevitably be in conflict with its own. The Spanish kingship was steadfast in this policy. It continued to appoint officials to the courtly-bureaucratic councils of state in the New World from amongst courtly and bureaucratic favorites trustworthy and loyal to it.

THE EXCLUSION OF THE COLONIALS
FROM HIGH ADMINISTRATIVE POSTS
(CIVIL AND RELIGIOUS)

The practice of exclusion of colonial-born Spaniards from all high bureaucratic posts in the new continent infuriated the colonials and set up a status distinction between themselves and those born in Spain. The colonials, who had left Spain in order to increase their status and power, having increased their power, now found themselves negatively statused when compared to the Spanish-born administrators. They were considered untrustworthy, uncouth, uncultured, and definitely beneath the continentals in manners and morality. Suddenly, those born in Latin America were not Spaniards, but "colonials" (*criollos*), and only those born and raised in the "cultured" atmosphere of Iberia were really Spaniards.

This is the well known *criollo* (Latin American-born)–*peninsulare* (Spanish-born) split which slowly grew up in the colonies. As we shall see, this split had much to do with the eventual movement for independence from Spain, for it forced a new identity upon the "colonials" and separated them off from the Spaniards as a reference group. In fact, *this split was the only reality category which forced a unity of identity to occur among the colonial-born Spaniards*, for this category differentiated all colonials from all Spanish-born, and forced upon the actually class-divided Latin Americans a common status for the first time. As is well known, when people are viewed as a group by another group, and stigmatized as if they are all the same, they—the stigmatized group—begin to act as if they have something in common, and in truth they do.

Thus, since in the eyes of the Spanish-born colonial governors and their lesser officials, both estate lords and landless citizens were considered to be a lower class of rustic colonials, similar feelings of status denial arose amongst both of the upper classes of Latin America, and for the first time, they were united in the mutual feelings of the newly forming common identity, "Latin American."

RAMIFICATIONS OF THE EXCLUSION OF THE COLONIALS FROM ADMINISTRATIVE OFFICES IN LATIN AMERICA: THE BEGINNINGS OF AN INDIGENOUS LATIN AMERICAN IDENTITY

Thus stigmatized, landed and landless Latin Americans alike began to develop a fierce tribalistic counterpoise to the status snub perpetrated by the snooty, Spanish-born governing officials, and in their attempt to deny the stigma of rusticity they toiled diligently to create their own myths of status and prestige.

First they asserted their superior valor and heroism, as opposed to the now decadent, restrained, and inhibited Spaniards, by harking back to the memory of the *conquistadores* from whom they sprang.

The myth of the man-on-horseback—the hero-on-horse-

back—was given a new twist. Now, the hero-on-horseback
—the soldier, the adventurer, "the man"—became the
venerated heritage of all the Latin Americans, upper and
lower class. The *conquistador* became the symbol of the
Latin American past—the proof of Latin American virility,
the model for Latin American identity, the factor that
distinguished the colonials from the obedient, ritualistic,
falsely pompous, bureaucratic Spanish governors.

And the *conquistador* was truly the most opportune
symbol the upper strata could have chosen around which
to fashion the new Latin American identity, for the lower
classes were attuned to just a symbol. The man-on-horseback was already their messianic hero, and the absentee
lords of the colonial upper strata were already identified
with this myth-image dating all the way back to the days
of the conquest, when the Indians were amazed and impressed with the seemingly super-human power of the war-
riors-on-horseback (the Indians had never seen a horse, so
the horseman became a mythical, demi-god figure to
them).*

Thus, the new Latin American identity-myth truly
served as a unifying symbol for all Latin Americans. It

---

* Whether these symbols were consciously chosen by the upper
classes to integrate and subordinate the lower classes, I do not know.
Later, after the wars of independence, the resurrection of the Indian past
and its glorification *was* consciously accomplished for this purpose—but
this was accomplished as much by the intellectuals and political radicals
seeking their own roots and identity (and their own biological identity,
I might add, since racial mixing had become so extensive that almost
everyone was of mixed parentage in some part of his lineage) as by the
ruling estate lords and commercial patriciate.

gave the status-denied upper strata their own convenient symbols of superiority to be used over/against the status denials fostered by the Spanish administrators; at the same time *it gave them their first feelings of unity with each other by creating a shared past* and blurring temporarily the status divisions existent between themselves in the present; and it provided a link between the Spanish-descended upper strata and the Indian and mestizo lower classes, which could now identify with the same symbols as the upper class and could thus share the same mythical past and a portion, at least of the same cultural identity.*

Features of the Indian past were brought in later to integrate the lower classes into the body politic and also to enhance the primitively virile symbol of masculinity that embellished the already existing symbol of the *conquistador*. The "*machismo*" complex was the result of this fusing of the invincible horseman-hero, the Spanish *conquistador*, and the primitive yet civilized Indian.

Its Old World roots stem from the Don Juan syndrome, the perversion of courtly chivalric love into conquest and seduction in the post-Moorish period, when the lords moved from the countryside to the cities and engaged in all manner of personal intrigue. It also stems from competition with the Moslems in terms of their

---

* See also the North American colonials after the War of Independence, who created a shared past of the "Founding Fathers," Washington-the-hero, Poor Richard's mottos, the frontier "pioneer spirit," the Constitution as sacred charter and symbol of American order and the Declaration of Independence as symbol of American spirit and liberty.

harem institution: masculine prowess was shown by the number of women a given man could "keep."

This Don Juan syndrome became part of the culture of post-Moslem, semi-feudal, city-centered Spain (and Italy). It was raised to the level of social cynosure in these countries (as the knightly style of life became dominant and the military roots of this class disappeared), and was brought to penultimate heights in Latin America when notions of primitive Indian virility and *conquistador* invincibility were added to this already grossly exaggerated style of masculinity. Thus, he who possesses *"machismo"* is at once a chivalric knight who knows the arts of courtly love, a caliph who has a thousand wives, a conquistador who conquers a whole new world, and a primitive whose blood runs fresh from his animal past.

This new Latin American identity was not fully fashioned or perpetuated until the war and post-war periods, of course, but the germs of the myths and symbols began to appear before the wars as pressures for separation from Spain mounted in the upper, status-denied classes, and dislocation increased amongst the dereified, negatively-privileged lower strata.

Thus, "the criollos (colonials), people of Spanish blood born in the Americas, were virtually excluded from the administration"[4] of the territories wherein they dwelt. But the legitimacy of the kingship was strong, and for many years the colonials did not question the king's authority. "Most of the complaints that were uttered (in the early years) were against maladministration by the king's servants, and corruption among the bureaucrats. The cry 'Long live the King and death to bad government' was frequently heard . . ."[5] But though the authority and legitimacy of the kingship was not questioned, the actual control of Latin American affairs was slowly passing to the colonials who both knew more about their own affairs and quite naturally took more of an active interest in the success of these affairs. Maladministration and corruption in the conduct of these affairs did not sit well with the colonials who could not but be hurt by the inefficient or corrupt administration of Latin American political, economic, or social activities.

24

THE PRESSURES FOR THE SEPARATION FROM THE SPANISH KINGLY-BUREAUCRATIC STATE BEGIN

THE LANDLESS COMMERCIAL CITY CLASS BEGINS TO MILITATE FOR INDEPENDENCE

With the movement of the estate lords to the cities, and their subsequent usurpation of political control of the entire territories involved, the political position of the landless city class greatly declined.

The landless, commercial city class had only two alternatives open to it for improving its position in the body politic: either it could increase its commercial enterprises and gain a large monetary base of power, and thus expand the prestige and power of its class as a class-for-itself (as its European counterparts were currently doing), or it could somehow gain land and merge with the estate-lord class, and thus gain prestige and power by transforming itself into this already positively privileged group (as had been the case in early post-feudal Europe, where the merchants systematically bought into and married into the knightly class).

But both these possibilities were blocked by the Spanish kingship, first through the Kingly monopoly on all commercial transactions in the Indies, and then through its rigid refusal to open the vast crown lands to further *encomienda* dispensation.

These latter policies did not sit well with the landless commercial class, for they were the major impediments to its political and economic expansion. The Spanish kingship was blocking the only two avenues of mobility available to the landless citizens, and the resentment engendered in them by the estate-lords' encroachments on their political domain slowly became deflected onto the Spanish kingship.

A further reason for directing this hostility towards the Spanish kingship was brought forward by the blocking of the only other possibility for mobility open to the city class—the ascension to bureaucratic office in the state structure.

This third alternative, that of expanding its political power gradually by controlling more and more of the offices of the bureaucratic state structure (a process accomplished throughout all Europe by the city classes, owing to their superior training in the letters and the law and their more practical business attitudes and procedures) was not open to the landless citizens of the

Latin American cities because they were "colonials," and only those born in Spain could hold these high posts. This restriction began to anger the landless citizens of the cities as their political position worsened under the expansionary pressures of the now city-dwelling estate lords.

The estate lords, for their part, cared little, in the beginning, for office-holding. They held most of the ruling power in the land anyway, through control of the city-centered parliaments and their countryside estates, and they were content to control the power—if not the actual offices—and pursue the new-found pleasures of the cities and the viceroyalty courts.

But to the landless city class, exclusion from high bureaucratic offices of state was a bitter pill to accept, for this had been their only avenue of political power extension. They had long occupied—by European estate-state precedent—the governing positions of their own cities, and had begun to exert quite a bit of power through the control of these offices.

They had begun to extend their power by occupying the lower regional offices as well, since the Spanish viceroyalty lacked men willing to spend time in backward rural districts living among the serfs or the remaining Indian villagers (except for the lower clergy, who were also drawn primarily from the landless city class, anyway). Even the youngest son of an estate lord, who often had difficulty in establishing his postion on the estate, disdained such a lowly office.

Thus it was that the landless city class had extended its power beyond the cities by occupying lesser civil and religious offices in lesser backwoods regions. The progress of this political power extension had been fairly regular, and the next obvious step for these aggressive, aspiring, upwardly mobile landless citizens should have been promotion into the upper bureaucratic ranks, but this logical next step—a step allowed in Spain to Spanish city-dwelling, landless citizens—was not forthcoming in Latin America.

The Spanish kingship systematically and rigidly forbade those who were born in the colonies, whether lord or merchant, to occupy key high offices.* Spaniards—strangers—often disinterested in the affairs of the colonies, merely acting in loyalty to the king or for personal political gain, hoping for their rapid return to Spain and disdaining the rusticity and lack of culture of the colonials, were appointed in their stead.

As mentioned, the estate lords cared little about this, since they did not desire to hold office. Bureaucratic procedures were boring to these semi-feudal, neo-knightly lords who were interested only in horsemanship, military exploits, the intrigue of the courts, and the pleasures of the cities. And, in fact, the lords liked the idea of being surrounded by Spaniards, for they brought the latest news

---

* There was a period in which the kingship conferred honorific posts upon estate lords to draw them to the cities in the hope of weakening their power by removing them from their serf-base, but these were never real offices and the kingship abandoned this practice after the lords had been drawn off the land.

and styles from Spain to the continent, they brought courtly grace and continental manners, they brought pomp and culture—in short, they allowed the Latin American estate lords to feel like true lords in a true court of real aristocrats. . . . What is a lord without a court and a king?

Therefore, in the period before the fall of the Spanish kingship (at the hands of Napoleon), the Latin American estate lords (although angered at their stigmatized, colonial, status-denied position) rather than breaking with the Spanish-born, kingly-controlled, disdainful viceroyalty entourages sent from Spain, idolized and emulated them in an attempt to remove their stigma and glean from them the culture and courtly grace of the continent.*

But though the estate lords cared little about the kingship's policy of appointing only the Spanish-born to high bureaucratic office, the landless citizens cared greatly, for their exclusion from these offices blocked their ability for political ascendency, and ended completely their chance for political expansion.

This class had already been blocked in its internal political expansion by the movement of the estate lords to the cities, and now it was being blocked once again, but this time by a power much farther away that was beginning to gain in its own domain.†

---

* Many of them actually traveled to Europe and spent time at the Spanish and Continental courts. This tradition of going to Europe to become cultured has been maintained to the present day among upper-class Latin Americans.

† Spain as a world power was giving way to France and England.

Blocked by the estate lords in its attempts at mobility and expansion, and with no hope of unseating them (lacking serf-armies or the wealth to find a paid professional army), the landless city class turned its wrath upon the Spanish kingship and its "foreign-born" surrogate court.

The seeds of hatred against the Spanish kingship had long festered in the commercial city class, for they had long harbored resentment against the kingly economic monopoly on all trade and commercial transactions in the colonies. Now that simmering resentment turned into open hostility. Their discontent was displaced onto the Spanish kingship—symbol of repression and stigmatization, of the usurpation of all affairs, political, economic, and social, by the foreign-born.

The Spanish kingship and its sophisticated viceroyalty courts in Latin America had created the status distinction "colonial" (meaning uncultured and uncouth) vs. "Spanish-born" (meaning cultured and suave); now this status distinction was to be used against it by the landless city class in its attempt to open the gates to the path of upward mobility once more.

Was it not the Spanish kingship that restricted all commercial enterprise within the colonies? Was it not the Spanish kingship that blocked all private trading transactions with the continent? Was it not the Spanish kingship that prevented indigenous office-holding in one's own land and stocked those offices with disinterested, unscrupulous, inefficient, and corrupt foreigners? And was it not the Spanish kingship that possessed enormous tracts of land—Crown and Church lands—that went unused but for the pleasure of foreigners?

The lands stood fallow and beckoned to the landless ones, precious products lined the docks of waiting trading lands . . . but the high posts of the land were held by the foreign-born.

And so, the first pressures toward separation from Spain were exerted by the landless city class in its attempt to expand its economic and political status and power—and no other class had yet joined in this struggle. But the landless class—swordless—was soon to be armed with that which was mightier than the sword, for the American and the French Revolutions, with their arsenal of liberal, enlightened, anti-kingly, pro-independence rhetoric was to supply them with the ideological slings and arrows necessary to penetrate to the hearts of all the classes of Latin America.

THE INTRODUCTION OF LIBERAL IDEOLOGY INTO LATIN AMERICA, AS CARRIED BY THE LANDLESS CITY CLASS

The enlightenment gave to the landless city class the ideological weapon that it needed to wage its war against the Spanish kingship and its foreign-born bureaucrats. The commercial city classes of Latin America grabbed onto the rallying cries of the commercial classes of Europe.

They began to make insolent speeches in the regional parliaments in attempt to persuade the estate lords to break with Spain. Their rhetoric was heated and passionate with the displaced anger of blocked mobility and status discrimination.

This wrath at first was turned solely upon the kingship and the foreign-born civic and religious bureaucrats, but it rapidly became extended against all "injustices"—just as European enlightenment rhetoric had. All oppression and venality came under attack, and the city commercial classes became the liberal defenders of the downtrodden, the outcast, and the oppressed.

But the actual goals of the landless ones were to gain land and wealth and status and power for themselves, rather than "justice for all." The brickbats they hurled against the church and the kingship were attempts to destroy these institutions' control over land and commerce, not create a utopian state of abundant redistribution. Yet, many honest liberal-humanitarian leaders emerged, of course, and these honest leaders began to frighten the estate lords (as well as the Spanish kingship) when they began attacking all injustice and inequality. They attacked not only the Church, but all venality, all sloth, all privilege. Thus, the estate lords came under attack, though usually by inference.

The passion of the city class and the power of the liberal-enlightenment rhetoric began to penetrate to the lower strata, and the bonds that had held the semi-feudal social structure together began to shatter. All who were oppressed—the serfs and the "dislocated ones"—were idealized and stirred beyond the bounds of their class position. The first rebellions began to occur—in Mexico, Hidalgo, the lawyer-priest, was the first to lead the Indian serfs into open rebellion against the lords.

But the beginnings of the success of the liberal leaders and the commercial class in stirring the populations at large toward independence from Spain and the kingship produced a violent reaction from the estate lords, who now saw the independence movement as a threat to their entire social reality and political supremacy.

The lords began to fear the power of the landless city class and its new-found weapon of words, but most of all they feared the power of the serfs and dislocated ones, for if the numbers of the serfs and the dislocated could be turned against them by the liberal leaders, their day would be done, their world would be over.

THE LORDLY REACTION

Thus did the estate-lords temporarily ally with the Spanish viceroyalties and Spanish-sent armies (as their counterparts had with the various kingships of Europe under similar circumstances). And the lords, with their serf-armies (at this point, most of the serfs still were loyal to the lords) combined with some Spanish troops, easily put down the poorly organized, almost spontaneous rebellions that erupted among the dislocated ex-serfs led by the liberal rhetoricians.

The landless city class was responsible for stirring up these rebellions, but as yet had no army, no force with which to back up its views. The lords, for their part, continued to back the Spanish kingship, and thus all attempts at independence were thwarted.

But, the landless city class did not quit its rhetoric, and its speeches grew longer and angrier and more desperate as its cause grew dimmer. And the seeds of the oratorical style that was to mark Latin American politics into the twentieth century were sown in the futility and desperation of the independence movement among the as yet powerless, landless citizens of the Latin American cities. The style of the rhetoric was to grow, while the content would shrink.

But, what the liberal rhetoric could not do, Napoleon temporarily did. The overthrow of the Spanish kingship by the liberal-minded Napoleonic state was to have profound consequences for Latin America.

NAPOLEON'S CONQUEST OF SPAIN AND ITS RAMIFICATIONS FOR LATIN AMERICA

Iberian rule over the New World had been unbroken for three hundred years, and the Spanish kingly state had been the dominant power of all Europe throughout most of its reign, but Spain was now yielding up its power to those purveyors of the commercial-industrial revolution that historical and structural circumstances had destroyed within her own body politic.* Soon, Spain was defeated, and for the first time could not back up its claim to the

* For the reasons behind Spain's decline, see Part I.

New World with military support. Suddenly the eternal strength and prestige of the Spanish kingship were broken.

The liberal leaders stepped up their campaign for independence—the crack in the dam was widened to a breach, but still the estate lords opposed total separation. But events in Spain changed their minds suddenly.

Under the influence of the Napoleonic code, a liberal-commercial faction raised its head for the last time and took control of Spain during Napoleon's reign and shortly thereafter. They attempted to de-feudalize Spain totally. The main thrust of their effort was directed at eliminating for once and for all those semi-feudal estates still under private lordly (or priestly) control. They were at once going to commercialize the land and reduce the autocratic class forever.

News of these intentions of the liberal Spanish government reached Latin America, and the estate lords quavered, for it was rumored that the same policy would be extended to the New World. The estate lords could not allow this, and for the first time they joined with the landless commercial class in opposing Spanish rule. The movement for independence had truly begun.

But Napoleon was driven from Spain, and the liberal reformers appeared as traitors spouting the ideas of the hated conqueror. The liberals were thus routed from office and a fierce reaction set in. Both State and Church became even more conservative than they had been before, and the rule of the *ancien régime* was reestablished with greater vigor and vigilance than ever in its past.* The commercial class and its liberal leaders were crushed forever, and a return to monopolistic economic control of Latin American raw materials was desperately sought.

Armies were sent to the New World—the resurrected, reactionary, declining Spanish kingly-bureaucratic state would fight on savagely to its last gasp in order to protect its dissipating life-line. And the Spanish army was still great, though Spain was not. And the war of independence would be many wars, for Spain would not yield easily, and the estate lords of Latin America would waver in their loyalties now that the conservative kingship had reassuringly returned to Spain.

But the tides of time could not be turned back fully in Latin America, for the liberal rhetoric had broken the bonds that held the serfs to the land, and their blood ran red in the sand as they fought for what they thought was independence from bondage, not from Spain. For the liberal rhetoric had stirred their dream of the return of their lost lands, and heroes-on-horseback stood ready to lead them on to the messianic goal. . . . But still Spain did not yield, and still the lords wavered, and the wars went on and on.

* The same occurred in Germany after Napoleon's withdrawal there.

Epilogue

The wars of independence dragged on inconclusively year after year, and the anarchy in the countryside increased year after year. The peasantry became even more separated from its allegiance to the land; the ranks of the dislocated ones swelled and began to burst the bonds of the entire social structure. The long wars created a situation where the entire population was converted to military attitudes. The indecisiveness of the wars produced a situation where armies in readiness assembled in the hills awaiting the turn of events.

When the wars ended, these armies remained in the hills and the anarchic banditry, which had plagued the countryside and become a permanent feature of Latin American life, now became militarized and professionalized. Bandit generals and their entourages came to control huge rural territories outside the authority of the estate-lords or the cities. These bandit generals came to be seen by the peasants as liberators—the dream of the messianic hero-on-horseback was renewed now with flesh and blood content. The bandit generals were charismatized by the peasantry and dislocated ones.

They attracted great followings—male and female—to their armed camps. In fact, they became so powerful that they represented a third force in the land, next to the estate-lords and the landless commercial citizens of the capital centers.

The wars had also set in motion another series of events. Since it was the city-dwellers—the liberals (imbued with the rhetoric of the enlightenment and the desire for economic and political gain)—who had vigorously pursued the wars and the separation from Spain, it was they who emerged as the heroes of the wars. All the heroes from Bolívar downward were city-dwellers from known "liberal" families. Thus when the wars ended, it was they who stood forth to create the nations. It was they who had intended the separation, it was they who had an ideology for separation, and it was they who desired a republican form of government over a kingship in any case. Therefore the task fell to them after the wars to create that which they stood for.

But, to do this, they would have to fight another war. For the estate-lords sat in the cities and the bandit heroes stood ready in the hills, once the Spanish kingship with its mantle of legitimacy and bureaucratic efficiency had been removed forever from the continent.

The estate-lords still controlled private armies of loyal peasants on their estates, and though their power was waning in the countryside, the union of various of the estates could still produce a formidable* army. The city-dwellers, too, could produce an army, since they still held

* Formidable by Latin American standards.

command posts in the armies of independence. These, however, had been temporary, and the liberation armies began to melt away rapidly after the wars so that the estate-lords came to hold a slight and growing military edge over the commercial city-dwellers. The bandit generals still waited in the hills.

The melting away of the armies of liberation commanded by the liberals was the signal to the estate-lords to begin again their struggle to penetrate and control the organs of state. Though the state structure was now shrouded in a liberal rhetoric, it began to take on the same institutional pattern it had had before the wars, with one exception. The legitimacy of the Spanish kingship had been removed. The viceroys and their bureaucratic entourage no longer controlled the organs and offices of state.

Competition for control of the state broke out nakedly now, for the symbols of the enlightenment were a transparent veil in Latin America where the semi-feudal class still held its power. The legitimacy of liberalism and its institutions of state and economic organization only became reified in territories where the classes carrying these values and institutions came to dominate the social structure—in Latin America this domination was ephemeral and disappeared rapidly after the wars. Thus the symbols of liberalism provided no legitimacy in Latin America and instead shrouded the issues and confused the populations.*

---

* They also confused liberal historians who failed to link ideology and rhetoric to their institutional bases.

But if it was true that liberalist enlightenment doctrine failed to provide legitimacy for the republics formed by the weak city classes, it is also true that the legitimacy system—namely, the kingship—which had been containing and controlling the semi-feudal estate-lord class no longer provided such legitimacy. Therefore, since no legitimacy was linked to any class or group competing in the political arena, political power and control of the organs of state was open to anyone who could get such power, by any means available. Bloodshed and naked force and unkept alliances are always the case in anarchic situations where no legitimations exist, and this is the situation which developed in Latin America.

This situation had been seething anyway even before the wars after the estate-lords had taken up permanent residence in the cities. But this process of cross-class and intraclass family feuding had been held in check to a large extent by the presence of the Spanish kingship—not only through its legitimating power but because of its control of the offices and administration of the state as well.

THE BLOOD FEUDS AND THE VIOLENCE

With the removal of the Spanish kingship in both its capacities as legitimator and administrator, and with the militarization of the entire region, and the accumulation of large hordes of dislocated peasants in the hills and in the cities, political struggle broke out into tremendous and unremitting violence—a violence that was to last for more than a century.*

The feuds broke out in the cities in earnest now, first between the estate-lords and the city-dwellers, then, as in the Italian and Spanish cities, between clans of the same class contending for the maintenance and inheritance of power as a permanent family right—not just the right of a given class.

As in Italy and Spain, the feuding took the form of using hired assassins and criminals, and often broke out into actual military combat.

The dislocated classes formed the bulk of the assassins and thieves who were professionalized by the feuding families. Peasant armies were gathered from the country-side by the estate-lords to fight their personal battles.† In the cities militias—as national armies remaining from the wars of independence—were created and mobilized by the commercial classes in an attempt to stave off the takeover by the estate-lords.

THE DICTATORS

The estate-lords and the city commercial classes thus fought it out after the wars. Blood ran in the cities. Political exiles became common.‡ Eventually—as mentioned—

---

* As in Italy and Spain in their city-state phases.

† In his unpublished article, "The Politics of Colombia," Arthur Vidich discusses the absorption and politicization of the lower classes by the upper classes who involved them in violence.

‡ Bolívar himself was exiled, returned, and was exiled again.

the class warfare degenerated into family warfare and
family feuding. The two contending classes began to
dissipate their strength and to become almost unable to
control the violence they had initiated. The situation got
to the point where too much blood flowed, where all
classes and families wanted to see the turmoil ended—at
least for awhile. To the bandit generals waiting in the hills
with their personal armies, this was their chance. The
estate-lords and city classes had dissipated themselves:
neither could restore order, neither could check the
bloodshed, and both had come to desire peace and rest.

Thus the bandit heroes rode into the capital cities. No
one opposed them, and everyone welcomed them, for
peace and rest were desired—for the time being.

Since the bandit heroes knew nothing of affairs of state,
competition for control of the state soon began again, and
the class and family conflicts erupted again. The bandit
heroes became embroiled in the feuds, siding with this or
that class—this or that family—but usually siding with
the estate-lords because of their own peasant origins and
their understanding and lingering respect for the lords and
their own desire to be a lord and live the knightly style of
life. They understood little of the rhetoric or institutions
of the liberals, and felt neither affinity nor respect for
them. Thus the bandit heroes—at first supreme dictators
enforcing order and peace—became henchmen and
lackeys of the estate-lords (and occasionally, in the later
periods, lackeys of the liberals),* but in any case, lackeys of
the contending families generally.

* This was especially true of Mexico.

Tiring of their role as peacemakers and policemen, and bored with state functions which they found themselves incapable of accomplishing, these bandit heroes after a few short years in power would ride off to the excitement of the hills, usually becoming bandits and empire lords again, terrorizing the countryside and making it unsafe for travelers, but not involving themselves in the office of state again.*

The cities would then be left to the feuding classes and families once more, bloodshed would break out again, and anarchy would reign in the land.

The cycle was repeated decade after decade. As soon as the bloodshed got out of hand, a bandit hero would be induced by one side or the other to enter the capital city and keep order. The other side would accept his presence because it too was glad to stop the bloodshed for a while.†

NEOCOLONIALISM

The wars of independence had still another effect on Latin American social and political organization.

That is, by severing its economic link with Spain, the wars left Latin America in debt to foreign powers.

During the wars large loans were taken by the Latin Americans from foreign powers wishing to break Spain's monopolistic hold on the raw materials produced in Latin

---

* Some were induced to return numerous times when city bloodshed got too out of hand.

† Fear that the dislocated ones would get totally out of hand and run wild—which happened occasionally—also motivated the acceptance of the *caudillo* type of dictatorship.

America. England, the young United States of America,
and other foreign powers made extensive loans to the
emerging nations. But when the wars ended, the republics
had no source of revenue with which to pay the enormous
debts incurred.

The landless commercial city classes attempted to set
up "liberal" republics, but from the outset were plagued
not only with political divisiveness but with economic
ruin as well, for the landless city classes had no source of
capital. Trade had been monopolized by Spain. Agriculture and mining production had been controlled by the
estate-lords. Imports rather than internal production had
provided consumption items. From what source could the
indigenous commercial classes gain the capital necessary
to pay off the foreign loans? From none.

Under this economic pressure, the liberal republics
went bankrupt, and the foreign powers became angry and
impatient and mistrustful of the young states.* The liberal politicans blustered and stalled and promised, but
failed to make good. Foreign powers came to distrust the
liberal politicians as all talk and no ability. The dream of
the enlightenment was dying in Latin America.

With their unmet loans as leverage, foreign powers
succeeded in extending their economic tentacles into
Latin America, for the economic monopoly of Spain had

---

* Alexander Hamilton's excellent handling of the United States debt
after the war of independence made the United States respectable in the
eyes of Europe. But the United States had industrial production and
capital available to allow for the rapid repayment of her war debts. The
Latin Americans had no such source of capital at hand.

been broken, and the raw materials of Latin America were open to the world market now.

But it was not the landless commercial city class that controlled the production and exportation of raw materials in Latin America. It was the estate-lords. They, though they lived in the cities, controlled this production through their serf-run estates. Overseers and later paid administrators saw to it that the raw materials were produced from the plantations and the mines. They had formerly been linked directly to the Spanish kingly bureaucratic state administering all exportation of raw materials. It was a simple jump to transfer this link to the new foreign powers who then—standing in Spain's place —administered and utilized the raw materials produced by the serfs of the great estates.

The foreign powers rapidly filled the gap left by Spain. They sent administrators, technically trained overseers, and mechanical equipment to Latin America. They built roads linking the estates and mines with the ports. They extended harbors and modernized loading and docking operations.* They did this more efficiently than Spain ever had, and linked the production of raw materials to the world market to a far greater extent than the Spaniards ever had.

This economic operation had startling political results for the entire social structure that was emerging in Latin America.

* Vidich discusses the underdeveloped countries in his unpublished lectures.

First of all, this economic expansion created a direct dependent link between Latin America and the foreign powers involved, exactly as that link had existed in the days of Spanish colonial domination, so that a kind of neocolonial structure emerged, replacing the colonial one that the Latin Americans had fought so hard to break.*

And secondly, a phenomenon occurred in Latin America—arising from this neocolonial relationship which has no parallel anywhere in Europe; that is, the linking of the semi-feudal estates to the world market as the producers of raw materials in Latin America furnished the estate-lords—as a class—with an external and enormous source of capital. Through this, it was the estate-lords— the aristocratic semi-feudal class—that became economically enriched and powerful, rather than the indigenous commercial class! In fact, the indigenous commercial class was cut off from any source of possible capital accumulation since production was once again controlled by the estate-lords and their serfs and administrators; the administration of trade was controlled by a foreign (now neocolonial) power; and the easy source of capital allowed the semi-feudal aristocrats to continue to import all items of subsistence and luxury.

Independence had altered little then, for estate-lords still dominated the land, and though Spain's monopoly had been broken, new foreign interests—rather than the

* Again the United States, through tariffs and indigenous industrial production, maintained its economic and political independence. But see the United States south! The South was as dependent on foreign markets as was Latin America!

indigenous commercial classes—still controlled trade and commercial enterprises. The economic hopes of the landless commercial classes were, thus, shattered.

Not only that, but the great political hopes of the commercial city classes were also shattered. For after the failure of the liberal politicians to pay off their economic debts, the foreign powers turned away from them completely and made their political alliances with the semifeudal class, since it was the semi-feudal class that was supplying the raw materials they wanted. The foreign powers were also aware that the commercial classes would try to inhibit trade and importations through tariffs and try to compete with them through indigenous production. They wanted none of this, nor did the semi-feudal class, for with their ready supply of capital from cash crops and mines they could easily purchase things from abroad.

From these elements emerged a permanent alliance between the foreign powers and the semi-feudal class of Latin America. Thenceforth, the foreign powers would deal exclusively with the estate-lords—back them politically, finance them indirectly, and when the chips were down, arm them and train them militarily to keep them in power and protect foreign interests there.

It is evident that the neocolonial relationship sustained the power of the semi-feudal class far beyond its time by supplying it with an endless source of capital. The neocolonial relationship by economic intent also inhibited the growth of an indigenous commercial and industrial class as a political entity within the emerging republics.

Both economic and military support were given the semi-feudal class by foreign powers—support they had never fully gained from the Spanish state. Meanwhile, the echoes of liberalism were fading from the Andean hills as the class that carried its institutions found itself armed with nothing but its own rhetoric. . . .

Bibliography

In reading over this bibliography, the reader will note that many books on the list are not specifically sources on Latin America. The reason for this is crucial, as it is the reason for the creation of this work.

The empirical data on Latin America have been available for almost a century—they are easily obtainable—and it was not my task to create another chronicle or statistical compilation. My task was to build a structural and theoretical framework in which the empirical facts of Latin America would appear meaningful. Thus the heavy reliance on theoretical, structural source materials.

Apter, David E., *China in Transition* (New York: Atheneum, 1955).
——, *The Politics of Modernization* (Chicago: University of Chicago Press, 1965).
Alexander, Robert J., *Prophets of the Revolution* (New York: Macmillan, 1962).
Almond, G. A., and J. S. Coleman, eds., *The Politics of Developing Areas* (Princeton, New Jersey: Princeton University Press, 1960).
Aristotle, *The Politics*, Benjamin Jowett, trans. (New York: Modern Library, 1943).
Bandelier, Adolf F. A., *An Archaeological Reconnaissance into Mexico* (Boston: Cupples and Hurd, 1895).
Bensman, Joseph, and Bernard Rosenberg, *Mass, Class, and Bureaucracy* (Englewood Cliffs, New Jersey: Prentice-Hall, 1963).

Berger, Peter L., and Thomas Luckman, *The Social Construction of Reality* (Garden City, New York: Doubleday, 1966).

Bottomore, Thomas B., *Elites and Society* (New York: Franklin Watts, 1964).

Chai, Ch'u, and Winberg, *The Changing Society of China* (New York: New American Library, 1960).

Childe, V. Gordon, *Man Makes Himself* (New York: New American Library, 1951).

Djilas, Milovan, *The New Class* (New York: Praeger, 1957).

Duffy, James, *Portugal in Africa* (Cambridge, Massachusetts; Harvard University Press, 1962).

Eisenstadt, Shmuel N., *The Political System of Empires* (New York: Macmillan, 1963).

Eserstad, *Essays in Comparative Institutions* (New York: Wiley, 1965).

Freyre, Gilberto, *The Masters and the Slaves* (New York: Alfred A. Knopf, 1956).

Hagen, Everett, *On The Theory of Social Change* (Homewood, Illinois: Dorsey Press, 1962).

Halpern, Manfred, *The Politics of Social Change in the Middle East and North Africa* (Princeton, New Jersey: Princeton University Press, 1963).

Harris, Marvin, *Patterns of Race in the Americas* (New York: 1964).

Hartz, Louis, *The Founding of New Societies* (New York: Harcourt, Brace & World, 1964).

Herring, Hubert C., *History of Latin America* (New York: Alfred A. Knopf, 1955).

Horowitz, Irving Lewis, *Revolution in Brazil* (New York: E. P. Dutton, 1964).

Institutional Reforms and Social Development Trends in Latin America (Washington, D.C., Inter-American Development Bank, 1963).

Janowitz, Morris, *The Military in the Political Development of New Nations* (Chicago: University of Chicago Press, 1964).

Johnson, John J., ed., *Continuity and Change in Latin America* (Stanford, California: Stanford University Press, 1964).

——, *The Military and Society in Latin America* (Stanford, California: Stanford University Press, 1964).

——, ed., *The Role of the Military in Underdeveloped Coun-*

tries (Princeton, New Jersey: Princeton University Press, 1962).

Kautsky, John H., *Political Change in Underdeveloped Countries* (New York: John Wiley, 1962).

Keller, Suzanne, *Beyond the Ruling Class* (New York: Random House, Inc., 1963).

Lagerkvist, Pär, *The Dwarf* (London: Chatto, 1953).

Lefevre, Georges, *The Coming of the French Revolution* (New York: Vintage, 1947).

Macridis, R. C., and Brown, B. E., eds., *Comparative Politics* (Homewood, Illinois: Dorscy, 1956).

Maier, Joseph Ben, and R. W. Weatherhead, *Politics of Change in Latin America* (New York: Praeger, 1964).

Mair, Lucy Philip, *New Nations* (Chicago: University of Chicago Press, 1963).

Mannheim, Karl, *Ideology and Utopia* (New York: Harcourt, Brace & World, 1936).

Mariéjol, Jean, *The Spain of Ferdinand and Isabella* (New Brunswick, New Jersey: Rutgers University Press, 1961).

Marx, Karl, *Economic and Philosophical Manuscripts of 1844*, Dirk J. Struik, ed. (New York: International Publishers, 1964).

———, and Freidrich Engels, *Selected Works*, Volumes I & II (New York: International Publishers, 1936).

McBride, George M., *Chile: Land and Society* (New York: American Geographical Society, 1936).

———, *Highlands of Bolivia* (New York: National Geographic Society, 1936).

———, *Mexico* (New York: 1936).

McCord, W., *The Springtime of Freedom* (Oxford: Oxford University Press, 1956).

Mills, C. Wright, *The Power Elite* (Oxford University Press, 1956).

———, *White Collar* (New York: Galaxy Books, 1956).

Moog, Clodonir Vianna, *Bandeirantes and Pioneers* (New York: George Braziller, 1964).

Mosca, Gaetano, *The Ruling Class*, Hanna Kahn, trans., and Arthur Livingston, ed. (New York: McGraw Hill, 1939).

Pendle, George, *A History of Latin America* (Baltimore: Penguin Books, 1963).

Petersen, William, *Population* (New York: Macmillan, 1961).

Pike, F. B., and D'Antonio, W. V., eds., *Religion, Revolution, and Reform* (New York: Praeger, 1964).

Rosenberg, Hans W., *Bureaucracy, Aristocracy, and Autocracy* (Cambridge, Massachusetts: Harvard University Press, 1958).

Rostow, Walt W., *Stages of Economic Growth* (Cambridge, England: Cambridge University Press, 1960).

Schumpeter, Joseph, *Imperialism and Social Classes*, H. Norden, trans. and ed. (New York: 1951).

———, *Capitalism, Socialism, and Democracy* (New York: Harper & Row, Publishers, 1950).

Scobie, James R., *Argentina, a City and a Nation* (New York: Oxford University Press, 1964).

Seton–Watson, Robert, *The East European Revolution* (New York: Praeger, 1951).

Silvert, Kalman H., *Reaction and Revolution in Latin America* (New Orleans, Louisiana: Hauser Press, 1961).

Simpson, Eyler N., *The Ejido: Mexico's Way Out* (Chapel Hill, North Carolina: University of North Carolina Press, 1937).

Webb, Hershel, *An Introduction to Japan* (New York: Columbia University Press, 1955).

Weber, Max, *Ancient Judaism*, H. H. Gerth and Don Martindale, eds. (Glencoe, Illinois: The Free Press, 1952).

———, *From Max Weber: Essays in Sociology*, H. H. Gerth and C. W. Mills, trans. and eds. (New York: Galaxy Books, 1958).

———, *General Economic History* (New York: Collier, 1927).

———, *Max Weber on the Methodology of the Social Sciences*, Shils and Finch, eds. (Glencoe, Illinois: The Free Press, 1949).

———, *On Law in Economy & Society*, Shils and Rheinstein, eds. (Cambridge, Massachusetts: 1954).

———, *The City*, Don Martindale and Gertrud Neuwirth, eds. (Glencoe, Illinois: The Free Press, 1958).

———, *The Religion of China*, H. H. Gerth, ed. and trans. (Glencoe, Illinois: The Free Press, 1951).

———, *The Religion of India*, H. H. Gerth and Don Martindale, trans. and eds. (Glencoe, Illinois: The Free Press, 1958).

———, *The Sociology of Religion*, E. Fischoff, trans. (Boston, Massachusetts: Beacon Press, 1963).

Notes

CHAPTER 1

1. Mariéjol: *The Spain of Ferdinand and Isabella.* *
2. *Ibid.*
3. *Ibid.*
4. *Ibid.*
5. *Ibid.*
6. Weber: *The City*

CHAPTER 2

1. Mariéjol.
2. *Ibid.*
3. *Ibid.*
4. *Ibid.*
5. *Ibid.*
6. *Ibid.*
7. *Ibid.*

CHAPTER 3

1. Weber; *see also* Aristotle: *Politics.*
2. *Ibid.*
3. Weber: "The Patrician City" in *The City; see also* Aristotle: "Oligarchy" in *Politics.*

4. Mariéjol.
5. *Ibid.*
6. Rosenberg: "The Prussian Experience" in *Bureaucracy, Aristocracy, and Autocracy.*
7. Mariéjol.
8. Rosenberg.
9. Mariéjol.
10. *Ibid.*
11. *Ibid.*
12. *Ibid.*
13. *Ibid.*
14. *Ibid.*
15. *Ibid.*

CHAPTER 4

1. Mariéjol.
2. *Ibid.*
3. *Ibid.*
4. *Ibid.*
5. *Ibid.*
6. Weber: on the Guelphs and the Ghibellines in Italy in *The City.*
7. Mariéjol.

* Complete citations for sources referred to in Notes appear in the Bibliography.

CHAPTER 5

1. Mariéjol.
2. *Ibid.*
3. *Ibid.*

CHAPTER 6

1. Mariéjol.
2. *Ibid.*
3. *Ibid.*
4. *Ibid.*
5. *Ibid.*
6. *Ibid.*
7. *Ibid.*
8. *Ibid.*
9. *Ibid.*
10. *Ibid.*
11. *Ibid.*
12. *Ibid.*
13. *Ibid.*
14. *Ibid.*
15. Rosenberg.
16. Mariéjol.
17. Rosenberg.
18. Mariéjol.
19. *Ibid.*
20. *Ibid.*
21. *Ibid.*
22. *Ibid.*
23. *Ibid.*
24. *Ibid.*
25. *Ibid.*
26. *Ibid.*

27. *Ibid.*
28. *Ibid.*
29. *Ibid.*
30. *Ibid.*
31. *Ibid.*

CHAPTER 7

1. Mariéjol.
2. *Ibid.*
3. *Ibid.*
4. *Ibid.*
5. *Ibid.*
6. *Ibid.*
7. *Ibid.*
8. *Ibid.*
9. *Ibid.*
10. *Ibid.*
11. *Ibid.*
12. *Ibid.*
13. *Ibid.*
14. *Ibid.*
15. *Ibid.*
16. *Ibid.*
17. *Ibid.*
18. *Ibid.*
19. *Ibid.*
20. *Ibid.*
21. *Ibid.*
22. *Ibid.*
23. *Ibid.*
24. *Ibid.*
25. *Ibid.*
26. *Ibid.*

CHAPTER 9

1. *Based on* Simpson: *The Ejido, Mexico's Way Out.*
2. Simpson.
3. *Ibid.*
4. *Ibid.*
5. *Ibid.*
6. *Ibid;* McBride: *Mexico.*
7. *Ibid.*
8. *Ibid.*
9. *Ibid.*
10. *Ibid.*

CHAPTER 10

1. McBride: *Chile: Land and Society* and *Mexico*
2. *Ibid.*
3. *Ibid.*
4. McBride: *Mexico.*
5. *Ibid.*
6. *Ibid.*
7. McBride: *Chile: Land and Society.*
8. *Ibid.*
9. *Ibid.*
10. McBride: *Mexico.*
11. *Ibid.*
12. McBride: *Chile: Land and Society* and *Mexico*
13. *Ibid.*
14. *Ibid.*
15. *Ibid.*
16. *Ibid.*

17. *Ibid.*
18. *Ibid.*

CHAPTER 11

1. McBride: *Mexico.*
2. *Ibid.*
3. *Ibid.*
4. *Ibid.*
5. *Ibid.*
6. *Ibid.*

CHAPTER 12

1. McBride: *Mexico.*
2. *Ibid.*
3. *Ibid.*
4. *Ibid.*
5. *Ibid.*
6. *Ibid.*
7. *Ibid.*
8. *Ibid.*
9. *Ibid.*
10. *Ibid.*
11. *Ibid.*
12. *Ibid.*
13. *Ibid.*
14. *Ibid.*
15. *Ibid.*
16. *Ibid.*
17. *Ibid.*
18. *Ibid.*
19. *Ibid.*
20. *Ibid.*

21. *Ibid.*
22. Simpson.
23. McBride: *Mexico.*
24. *Ibid.*
25. *Ibid.*
26. *Ibid.*
27. *Ibid.*
28. *Ibid.*
29. *Ibid.*
30. *Ibid.*

CHAPTER 13

1. McBride: *Mexico.*
2. *Ibid.*
3. McBride: *Mexico* and *Chile: Land and Society.*
4. *Ibid.*
5. *Ibid.*
6. *Ibid.*
7. *Ibid.*
8. *Ibid.*
9. *Ibid.*
10. *Ibid.*
11. *Ibid.*

CHAPTER 14

1. McBride: *Mexico*
2. *Ibid.*
3. *Ibid.*

CHAPTER 15

1. Freyre: *The Masters and the Slaves.*

2. *Ibid.*
3. Vidich: "The Politics of Columbia," unpublished article, New School for Social Research.
4. Harris: *Patterns of Race in the Americas.*

CHAPTER 16

1. McBride: *Mexico* and *Chile: Land and Society.*
2. *Ibid.*
3. *Ibid.*
4. *Ibid.*
5. *Ibid.*
6. *Ibid.*
7. *Ibid.*
8. *Ibid.*
9. *Ibid.*
10. *Ibid.*
11. *Ibid.*
12. *Ibid.*
13. *Ibid.*
14. Freyre.

CHAPTER 17

1. Pendle: A *History of Latin America.*
2. Herring: *History of Latin America.*
3. Phipps: "Some Aspects of the Agrarian Question in Mexico," in Simpson.
4. *Ibid.*

5. Pendle.
6. McBride: *Mexico*.
7. McBride: *Mexico* and *Chile: Land and Society*.
8. *Ibid.*
9. Pendle.
10. McBride: *Mexico* and *Chile: Land and Society*.
11. Herring.
12. Weber: *The City* and *The Sociology of Religion*.

CHAPTER 18

1. McBride: *Mexico*.
2. *Ibid.*
3. *Ibid.*
4. *Ibid.*
5. McBride: *Mexico* and *Chile: Land and Society*.
6. *Ibid.*
7. McBride: *Mexico*.
8. *Ibid.*
9. *Ibid.*
10. McBride: *Chile: Land and Society*.

CHAPTER 19

1. McBride: *Chile: Land and Society*.
2. McBride: *Chile: Land and Society*.
3. *Ibid.*

CHAPTER 20

1. McBride: *Mexico* and *Chile: Land and Society*.
2. *Ibid.*
3. *Ibid.*
4. *Ibid.*
5. *Ibid.*

CHAPTER 21

1. McBride: *Chile: Land and Society*.
2. *Ibid.*
3. *Ibid.*
4. *Ibid.*
5. Vidich.
6. Pendle.

CHAPTER 22

1. McBride: *Mexico*.
2. McBride: *Chile: Land and Society*.
3. *Ibid.*
4. *Ibid.*
5. *Ibid.*

CHAPTER 23

1. Pendle: *History of Latin America*.
2. *Ibid.*
3. *Ibid.*
4. *Ibid.*
5. *Ibid.*

Index

320.9 Glassman, Ronald
G   M.

Political
history of
Latin America

12546

DATE			

561